Notre-Dame's Dark Secrets

Unveiling the Mysteries Unearthed by the

GW01086970

Louis Martin

Published by At Triangle Inc.

Publisher Information

Published b At-Triangle Corporation

Chiba, Japan

Disclaimer

This book is a work of nonfiction. While every effort has been made to ensure accuracy, some interpretations of historical events and cultural insights may reflect the author's personal perspective.

First Edition: November 2024

Table of Contents

Foreword

Few landmarks in the world evoke as much awe and reverence as Notre-Dame de Paris. Rising majestically above the Seine, this Gothic masterpiece has stood for centuries as a symbol of faith, resilience, and the enduring spirit of humanity. It has witnessed revolutions, royal coronations, and wars, silently chronicling the passage of time while inspiring countless visitors and artists with its ethereal beauty.

But in April 2019, this iconic cathedral captured global attention for a very different reason. As flames consumed its roof and brought the centuries-old spire crashing down, the world watched in collective heartbreak. For many, the fire was a tragedy—a loss of irreplaceable history and culture. Yet, in its ashes, Notre-Dame began to reveal something extraordinary.

Hidden chambers, forgotten artifacts, and structural mysteries buried beneath layers of time suddenly came into focus. The fire, while devastating, unearthed secrets that had remained concealed for centuries. From its symbolic gargoyles to its enigmatic stained glass windows, Notre-Dame seemed to whisper stories waiting to be told.

This book invites you to journey through the hidden history of Notre-Dame, exploring the mysteries it has safeguarded and the revelations brought to light by the fire. You will uncover not just the triumphs of its builders but also the secrets encoded in its stones, the legends that surround it, and the profound lessons it continues to teach us about human ingenuity and resilience.

Whether you are a lover of history, architecture, or the enduring magic of storytelling, this book promises to take you deeper into the heart of Notre-Dame than ever before. Together, let us discover how a monument forged in the Middle Ages continues to illuminate the present and inspire the future.

Welcome to the untold story of Notre-Dame de Paris.

Louis Martin
November 2024

Introduction: The Eternal Symbol of Paris

1.Notre-Dame's Place in Parisian Life

Notre-Dame de Paris is more than a cathedral; it is the heartbeat of Paris. For centuries, it has stood as a silent witness to the lives of Parisians, transcending its religious function to become an inseparable part of the city's identity. Its soaring towers and intricate stonework are not merely architectural feats but symbols of resilience, faith, and the enduring spirit of Paris. To truly understand Notre-Dame's significance, one must delve into its profound connection to the daily lives, dreams, and struggles of those who have walked its shadowed plazas and crossed the bridges leading to its majestic facade.

To the average Parisian, Notre-Dame is as familiar as the Seine. Its silhouette is etched into the city's skyline, a comforting presence visible from countless angles. It anchors not only the physical layout of Paris but also the emotional and cultural geography of its people. In moments of triumph and despair, Notre-Dame has been a place of solace, celebration, and reflection. It is the stage upon which the city's most defining moments have unfolded, from royal processions to revolutions, and from jubilant victories to quiet personal prayers. The stones of Notre-Dame have absorbed the tears, whispers, and laughter of generations, creating an intangible bond between the structure and its people.

In the medieval era, Notre-Dame was the bustling heart of the Île de la Cité, the central island of Paris. This was not just the religious epicenter of the city but a vibrant hub of commerce and community life. The square before the cathedral was alive with activity: merchants selling wares, entertainers captivating crowds, and children weaving between the legs of passersby. The bells of Notre-Dame rang out over the city, marking not only the hours of the day but the rhythms of life. Their sound was a constant presence, reminding everyone of the greater, unchanging order amidst the chaos of daily life.

The cathedral's relationship with Parisians goes beyond its physical presence. Its stories and legends have woven themselves into the folklore of the city. Generations of children grew up hearing tales of the grotesque gargoyles perched on Notre-Dame's towers. Some believed they were protectors of the city, warding off evil spirits with their menacing visages. Others whispered that these stone creatures came to life under the light of the full moon, roaming the streets of Paris to ensure the city's safety. These myths, passed down through the years, have given Notre-Dame a sense of mystery and wonder, endearing it even further to the hearts of Parisians.

The cathedral's influence extended far beyond the realm of faith, embedding itself into the secular consciousness of the city. During the French Revolution, when religion was under siege, Notre-Dame became a powerful symbol of both rebellion and resilience. It was deconsecrated, its treasures looted, and its statues decapitated, yet it stood firm. Its very survival became a testament to the enduring spirit of Paris. As revolutions came and went, the cathedral remained, a silent reminder of the city's ability to weather change and upheaval.

In modern times, Notre-Dame has continued to be a cornerstone of Parisian identity, a place where history and the present intersect. For tourists, it is a must-see landmark, but for Parisians, it is a living, breathing part of their daily lives. Couples stroll hand in hand along the Seine, their conversations punctuated by the sight of the cathedral's towers. Artists gather on its steps, sketching its intricate details or simply soaking in its majesty. Street performers sing and play in its shadow, adding their own notes to the symphony of life that surrounds it. Even those who do not step inside its doors feel its presence, a reassuring constant in a rapidly changing world.

Notre-Dame also holds a unique place in the quieter, personal moments of Parisian life. It is where people come to mark milestones—baptisms, weddings, and funerals. It is where they light candles in moments of grief or gratitude, seeking comfort in its hallowed halls. For many, it is not the grandeur of the cathedral that resonates most, but its ability to make them feel connected to something larger than themselves. It is a sanctuary not just from the noise of the city but from the chaos of life.

The fire of 2019 only deepened this connection. As flames devoured its roof and brought down its beloved spire, the people of Paris gathered in disbelief. The sight of Notre-Dame ablaze was a collective heartbreak, a moment that felt almost surreal. Yet, as the ashes settled, something remarkable happened. Parisians rallied around their cathedral, proving that Notre-Dame was far more than a building. It was a symbol of their shared history, their resilience, and their unwavering spirit. The crowds that gathered on the banks of the Seine sang hymns, their voices rising to fill the void left by the bells that no longer rang. In those moments, the bond between Paris and Notre-Dame was stronger than ever.

Today, as the cathedral undergoes its meticulous restoration, it continues to occupy a central place in the life of the city. Its absence from daily life has only served to underscore its importance. For Parisians, the sight of scaffolding around Notre-Dame is not just a reminder of what was lost, but a symbol of hope and renewal. It is a testament to their determination to preserve their heritage, not just for themselves but for future generations.

Notre-Dame's place in Parisian life is not just about its physical presence or its historical significance. It is about the way it makes people feel. It is a reminder of the power of beauty, faith, and community. It is a place where the past and present coexist, where every stone tells a story and every shadow holds a memory. For Parisians, Notre-Dame is not just a part of their city—it is a part of their soul.

As the restoration continues and the world watches, Notre-Dame remains a beacon of hope and resilience, a symbol of everything that makes Paris extraordinary. And for the people of this city, it will always be more than a cathedral. It will be a home, a sanctuary, and a timeless witness to the story of Paris.

2. The Cathedral's Global Significance

Notre-Dame de Paris is not merely a symbol of Paris or France; it is an emblem of shared human heritage. Over centuries, it has transcended its geographic location to become a universal icon, a structure that resonates deeply with people from all walks of life and corners of the globe. Its significance reaches beyond its architectural grandeur or its religious importance. Notre-Dame represents resilience, creativity, and the enduring human spirit, qualities that speak to a world far beyond the Île de la Cité.

What makes Notre-Dame so universally revered? Perhaps it is because, while it is distinctly Parisian, it embodies values and aspirations that are fundamentally human. When one gazes at its towering spires or walks beneath its cavernous arches, it becomes clear that Notre-Dame is more than stone and glass. It is a testament to what humanity can achieve when driven by a vision that stretches beyond the limitations of the present. Its construction began in the 12th century, at a time when resources were scarce, tools were rudimentary, and life was often brutal. Yet, against all odds, it rose to become a beacon of hope and beauty.

Throughout history, Notre-Dame has inspired awe and wonder not just in Parisians but in travelers and thinkers from every part of the world. For centuries, it was one of the first landmarks that greeted visitors arriving in Paris. Merchants, pilgrims, and scholars who came to the city often spoke of their first glimpse of Notre-Dame as a transformative experience. The cathedral's silhouette, reflected in the waters of the Seine, seemed to welcome them into a city where the sacred and the profane, the historical and the contemporary, merged seamlessly.

Victor Hugo's 19th-century novel *Notre-Dame de Paris*—known in English as *The Hunchback of Notre-Dame*—amplified the cathedral's global appeal. Hugo brought Notre-Dame to life as more than a backdrop; it became a central character in its own right, embodying the tension between beauty and decay, tradition and progress. The novel captured the imagination of readers around the world, many of whom had never set foot in Paris. Through Hugo's vivid descriptions, they could hear the toll of the cathedral's bells, feel the cool shadows of its interior, and marvel at the intricate carvings of its gargoyles.

Hugo's work did more than immortalize Notre-Dame in literature—it galvanized efforts to preserve the cathedral. By the early 19th century, Notre-Dame had fallen into disrepair, a relic of a bygone era in a city hurtling toward modernization. The novel sparked a movement to restore the cathedral, led by architect Eugène Viollet-le-Duc. The restoration project not only saved Notre-Dame but also set a precedent for preserving historical monuments worldwide. In this way, the cathedral became a model for how societies could honor their past while embracing the future.

Notre-Dame's influence extends beyond the realm of art and literature. It has become a universal symbol of faith, resilience, and unity. During pivotal moments in history, its bells have rung out to mark both celebration and sorrow. In 1944, as Paris was liberated from Nazi occupation, the bells of Notre-Dame pealed with a jubilance that echoed around the world. Similarly, when tragedy struck—such as the terror attacks on Paris in 2015—people from across the globe gathered in the shadow of the cathedral, lighting candles and seeking solace.

In the modern era, Notre-Dame has become a magnet for millions of visitors annually. Tourists from every continent flock to its doors, drawn by its history, its art, and its aura. For some, it is a pilgrimage to a sacred site; for others, it is an opportunity to witness a masterpiece of human ingenuity. The diversity of its visitors reflects its universal appeal. Standing in the square before the cathedral, one can hear a cacophony of languages, all united by the shared experience of beholding Notre-Dame.

Yet, the cathedral's global significance goes beyond its physical presence. Notre-Dame has become a touchstone in the collective imagination, appearing in films, books, and even political discourse. Its image is instantly recognizable, whether it is depicted in animated films like *The Hunchback of Notre Dame* or as a backdrop to global events. It serves as a reminder that certain symbols transcend their origins to become part of a shared cultural vocabulary.

The fire of April 15, 2019, underscored Notre-Dame's place in the global consciousness. As flames engulfed the cathedral's roof and toppled its iconic spire, the world held its breath. The sight of Notre-Dame burning was a collective heartbreak, a moment of shared grief that transcended borders. Social media was flooded with images and messages from people in every corner of the globe, expressing their sorrow and solidarity. Donations poured in, from billionaires to ordinary citizens, all united by a common desire to see Notre-Dame restored.

The fire also revealed something profound: Notre-Dame does not belong to any one country or culture. It is a global treasure, a symbol of our shared history and humanity. The restoration project that followed became an international effort, with architects, artisans, and historians from around the world contributing their expertise. The process of rebuilding Notre-Dame is not just about restoring a building; it is about reaffirming the values it represents: resilience, creativity, and the enduring power of community.

As the world looks toward the future, Notre-Dame continues to serve as a beacon of hope and inspiration. It reminds us that while we may come from different places, speak different languages, and hold different beliefs, there are certain symbols that unite us. Notre-Dame is one of those symbols—a testament to the beauty of what we can achieve together.

When visitors stand beneath its vaulted ceilings or gaze up at its rose windows, they are not just witnessing a piece of history; they are participating in it. They are part of a continuum that stretches back centuries and will extend far into the future. This is the true significance of Notre-Dame: it is not just a monument to the past but a bridge to the future, a reminder of what we share as human beings.

In a world that often feels divided, Notre-Dame stands as a symbol of unity. It speaks to the best of who we are and what we can aspire to be. Its significance is not limited to its role as a cathedral or a tourist destination. Notre-Dame is, and always will be, a universal icon—a reminder that some things are bigger than any one person, place, or time.

3.The Day the Flames Rose: A Moment of Shock

April 15, 2019, began like any other spring day in Paris. The Seine flowed gently beneath the bridges, cafés bustled with their usual charm, and Notre-Dame stood steadfast at the heart of the city, as it had for centuries. But by the evening, the world would witness a tragedy so shocking and surreal that it seemed almost impossible to believe. The fire that engulfed Notre-Dame de

Paris on that fateful day was more than an event; it was a collective heartbreak, a moment that would forever mark the history of a city, a country, and the world.

The first signs of trouble appeared late in the afternoon. Tourists exploring the cathedral's iconic interior and climbing its ancient towers noticed the faint smell of smoke. At first, it was dismissed as a quirk of the old building, perhaps dust from the ongoing restoration work. But then, a plume of smoke began to rise into the sky, faint but unmistakable, curling against the evening light. Within minutes, the situation escalated from curious to catastrophic. Flames erupted with alarming ferocity, licking hungrily at the scaffolding that had been erected for repairs. The medieval timbers of the attic, some of which dated back nearly a millennium, provided perfect fuel for the fire.

News of the blaze spread rapidly, first through Paris and then to the rest of the world. Social media lit up with images and videos of the cathedral consumed by fire, its iconic spire shrouded in thick, dark smoke. For many, the sight was too devastating to comprehend. Notre-Dame was not just a building; it was a symbol, a repository of history, art, and faith. To see it burning felt like witnessing the destruction of a piece of humanity itself.

As firefighters raced to the scene, crowds began to gather along the banks of the Seine. The mood was a mixture of disbelief and helplessness. People held their breath, hoping the fire could somehow be contained, even as they watched the flames spread with relentless determination. When the spire—the elegant, skyward-reaching pinnacle added during the 19th-century restoration—began to sway, the crowd gasped audibly. Moments later, it collapsed in a shower of embers, a sight that would be replayed endlessly on news broadcasts around the world. It was as though the soul of Notre-Dame had fallen with it.

Inside the cathedral, the situation was dire. Firefighters fought valiantly to save the structure, risking their lives as they worked under the collapsing roof. The heat was intense, the air thick with smoke and ash. Water from their hoses cascaded onto the flames, hissing and steaming as it met the inferno. Their primary goal was clear: to save the main body of the cathedral, the iconic twin towers, and as much of the priceless art and relics as possible. Among these treasures was the Crown of Thorns, believed by many to have been worn by Christ during his crucifixion. Miraculously, it was salvaged, thanks to the efforts of brave first responders and clergy who formed a human chain to pass the relics to safety.

As the fire raged on, Parisians began to sing. Gathered in somber clusters along the Seine, they lifted their voices in hymns and prayers. The haunting strains of "Ave Maria" filled the night air, a poignant counterpoint to the crackling of the flames. It was a moment of unity and defiance, a testament to the deep emotional connection between the city and its cathedral. For those present, it was as if their voices could somehow protect Notre-Dame, wrapping it in a collective embrace.

Across the globe, the images of Notre-Dame in flames evoked a similar sense of loss and solidarity. Political leaders, cultural figures, and ordinary citizens expressed their shock and sadness. Statements poured in from every corner of the world, emphasizing the cathedral's universal importance. Notre-Dame was not just a monument of French heritage; it was a symbol of human creativity and perseverance, a treasure that belonged to everyone.

The fire burned for hours, and by the time it was finally extinguished, the damage was staggering. The roof was gone, reduced to smoldering rubble, and the famous "Forest," the intricate wooden framework that had supported the roof for centuries, was no more. The nave lay exposed to the sky, its stone walls blackened with soot. Yet, amidst the destruction, there were glimmers of hope. The twin towers, the great organ, and the magnificent rose windows, though damaged, had survived. Notre-Dame, battered but not broken, had endured once again.

In the days that followed, the fire became a unifying moment for France and the world. Donations for the restoration poured in at an unprecedented pace, from billionaires pledging millions to individuals contributing what little they could. Architects, historians, and artisans from across the globe offered their expertise, eager to help rebuild what had been lost. The French president, Emmanuel Macron, vowed that Notre-Dame would rise again, sparking a renewed sense of determination and pride among the people.

For many, the fire was a stark reminder of the fragility of human achievement. Notre-Dame had stood for over 850 years, surviving wars, revolutions, and neglect, only to be brought to its knees by a single spark. Yet, it also served as a powerful symbol of resilience. The outpouring of grief and support demonstrated that Notre-Dame was more than a historical artifact; it was a living part of the world's collective soul.

The events of April 15, 2019, remain etched in the memories of those who lived through them, a day when the world stopped to mourn the loss of something irreplaceable. But they also marked the beginning of a new chapter for Notre-Dame. The fire, while devastating, brought the cathedral into sharp focus, reminding people everywhere of its profound significance. It is a testament to humanity's ability to create, to endure, and to come together in times of crisis.

Notre-Dame's story did not end with the fire; it continues to unfold. The scars of that day are still visible, but they are also a source of strength. They are a reminder of what was lost and of what remains, of the challenges ahead and the hope that drives us forward. The day the flames rose will forever be a moment of shock and sorrow, but it will also stand as a testament to the enduring spirit of Notre-Dame and the people who cherish it.

4.Why the World Watched: The Media Frenzy

The fire at Notre-Dame de Paris on April 15, 2019, was not just a tragedy for Paris or France—it was an event that transfixed the entire globe. Within minutes of the first flames licking the cathedral's ancient wooden beams, news began to spread. Social media feeds filled with photos and videos, live broadcasts captured the collapse of the spire, and headlines across continents screamed the devastating news. For a few hours, it seemed as though the whole world was focused on a single point: the burning heart of Paris.

But why did this event grip the attention of billions? Fires occur every day, even at historic landmarks, and tragedies often compete for headlines. Yet, Notre-Dame's fire stood apart, commanding an extraordinary level of global engagement. To understand why, one must delve into the cultural, emotional, and symbolic significance of the cathedral and how the power of modern media transformed the event into a shared, worldwide experience.

At its core, Notre-Dame represents more than just a building; it is a universal symbol. Its towering spires and intricate gargoyles have graced countless postcards, films, and books, making it instantly recognizable even to those who have never set foot in Paris. The cathedral's story is deeply intertwined with the cultural identity of the Western world. For many, it is a reminder of Europe's medieval past, a time when faith, art, and ingenuity converged to create architectural masterpieces that still stand as testaments to human achievement.

When the flames erupted that evening, Notre-Dame became a metaphor for fragility—a stark reminder that even the most enduring symbols are not invincible. The sight of the spire collapsing into a sea of fire struck a chord in viewers everywhere. It was as if a part of humanity's shared history was crumbling before their eyes, and the immediacy of modern media allowed that moment to be experienced in real-time by millions.

News outlets quickly mobilized, flooding their channels with images and reports from the scene. Helicopter footage showed the cathedral engulfed in smoke, the glow of the fire illuminating the Parisian skyline. On-the-ground reporters captured the reactions of stunned onlookers, their faces etched with disbelief and sorrow. These images were broadcast worldwide, creating a visceral connection between viewers and the tragedy unfolding thousands of miles away.

Social media amplified this connection exponentially. Platforms like Twitter, Facebook, and Instagram became inundated with posts about Notre-Dame, as individuals shared their grief, memories, and disbelief. The hashtag #NotreDame trended globally within minutes, with millions of tweets pouring in from every corner of the earth. For many, the act of sharing their thoughts and emotions online became a way to process the shock and sadness they felt. The fire became not just an event but a collective experience, as people turned to digital spaces to mourn together.

One of the most striking aspects of the media frenzy was the sheer variety of voices that emerged. Politicians, celebrities, historians, architects, and ordinary citizens all joined the conversation. French President Emmanuel Macron addressed the nation that very evening, his words carrying an urgency and sorrow that resonated far beyond France's borders. Leaders from around the world offered their condolences, highlighting the cathedral's universal significance. Hollywood stars posted photos of their visits to Notre-Dame, recalling personal memories that mirrored those of countless others. Historians shared insights into the cathedral's construction and cultural impact, while architects lamented the potential loss of one of the world's great Gothic masterpieces.

The media coverage was not merely a reflection of public interest; it also shaped how the event was perceived. The continuous stream of updates created an almost cinematic narrative, complete with heroes—firefighters battling against impossible odds—and moments of triumph, such as the rescue of the Crown of Thorns and other irreplaceable relics. This narrative gave viewers a sense of emotional investment, as if they were part of the unfolding drama. The fire at Notre-Dame was no longer just a news story; it had become a global spectacle.

Yet, the media frenzy also sparked debates about priorities and values. While many mourned the damage to Notre-Dame, others questioned why the destruction of a building—however iconic—received more attention than other pressing global issues. Some pointed out the stark contrast between the millions of dollars pledged for Notre-Dame's restoration within hours of the fire and the lack of similar urgency for humanitarian crises. These critiques, widely discussed online and in editorial columns, underscored the complex role of media in shaping public discourse and attention.

Despite these controversies, the coverage of the fire revealed something profound about humanity's capacity for connection. The outpouring of emotion, support, and solidarity transcended borders, languages, and cultures. People who had never visited Notre-Dame, who perhaps had never even heard of it before that day, felt compelled to contribute to its restoration. Donations flowed in from every corner of the globe, from billionaires pledging vast sums to children donating their pocket money. This collective response was a testament to the power of media to not only inform but also inspire action.

In the days and weeks following the fire, the media continued to play a pivotal role. Documentaries and in-depth articles explored the history and significance of Notre-Dame, educating audiences about its cultural and architectural importance. Photographers captured haunting images of the cathedral's charred interior, juxtaposing the devastation with moments of hope, such as the intact altar cross gleaming amid the rubble. These stories kept the world's attention focused on Notre-Dame, ensuring that the momentum for its restoration did not wane.

The fire at Notre-Dame was, in many ways, a perfect storm for the media age. It combined an iconic location, a dramatic and visually arresting event, and a profound emotional resonance that transcended cultural boundaries. But beyond the headlines and hashtags, it revealed something deeper about the human experience. In a world often divided by politics, geography, and ideology, the burning of Notre-Dame became a moment of unity. It reminded us that certain symbols, like Notre-Dame, belong not to one nation but to all of humanity.

As the restoration of Notre-Dame continues, the media's role in shaping its story remains crucial. The images of the fire and its aftermath are now etched into the collective memory, a reminder of both loss and resilience. And while the flames may have subsided, the story of Notre-Dame—its history, its significance, and its ability to bring people together—continues to captivate the world.

Chapter 1: The Rise of Notre-Dame : From Foundations to Glory

1.The Visionaries Behind Notre-Dame

In the 12th century, Paris was a city on the rise. The Île de la Cité, a bustling island in the Seine, was the nucleus of political, economic, and religious life in France. The reigning monarch, King Louis VII, had grand ambitions for his capital, seeking to elevate it as a center of power, faith, and culture. Central to this vision was the construction of a cathedral that would not only rival but surpass all others—a structure so grand and awe-inspiring that it would embody the glory of God and the growing prestige of Paris. Thus began the story of Notre-Dame de Paris, a masterpiece brought to life by the visionaries who dared to dream beyond the limits of their time.

The seeds of Notre-Dame were planted by Maurice de Sully, the Bishop of Paris. Born to humble beginnings in Sully-sur-Loire, Maurice rose to prominence through his intellect, charisma, and unwavering dedication to his faith. As Bishop, he was acutely aware that the existing cathedral, Saint-Étienne, was inadequate for the needs of a growing city and an increasingly powerful Church. Saint-Étienne, though historic, was a patchwork of outdated styles, lacking the unity and grandeur required to reflect the ambitions of Paris.

Maurice envisioned something extraordinary—a new cathedral that would serve as both a house of worship and a symbol of divine and earthly authority. His vision was rooted in the emerging Gothic style, which was revolutionizing architecture across Europe. This new style, characterized by soaring verticality, pointed arches, and expansive stained-glass windows, was not just an aesthetic choice; it was a theological statement. Gothic architecture sought to draw the eyes—and the soul—heavenward, creating a physical space that reflected the majesty of God.

In 1163, under Maurice's leadership and with the blessing of King Louis VII, the cornerstone of Notre-Dame was laid. It was an ambitious undertaking, one that would span nearly two centuries and involve countless artisans, laborers, and architects. Yet, despite the enormity of the task, Maurice de Sully's unwavering commitment set the tone for the project. His vision extended beyond the physical structure; he sought to create a sacred space that would unite the people of Paris and inspire generations to come.

While Maurice provided the spiritual and conceptual foundation for Notre-Dame, the realization of his vision fell to a series of master builders, whose ingenuity and artistry transformed his dream into reality. These architects, though often unnamed and uncelebrated, were the true heroes of Notre-Dame. Working with rudimentary tools and under the constant pressure of a monumental task, they pushed the boundaries of what was architecturally possible.

One of the most remarkable aspects of Notre-Dame's construction was the sheer scale of innovation it demanded. The use of ribbed vaults allowed the builders to construct higher ceilings while reducing the weight borne by the walls. This innovation made it possible to incorporate large stained-glass windows, flooding the interior with light and color. Flying buttresses, a groundbreaking feature at the time, were introduced to provide additional structural support, enabling the cathedral's walls to soar to unprecedented heights. These architectural advancements were not merely functional; they were a testament to the visionaries' relentless pursuit of beauty and perfection.

The labor required to build Notre-Dame was immense, involving a vast network of workers from diverse backgrounds. Stonecutters, masons, carpenters, and blacksmiths each played a vital role, their collective effort shaping every detail of the cathedral. The construction process was a living embodiment of community and faith, with entire generations of families dedicating their lives to the project. For many of these workers, the act of building Notre-Dame was itself an act of devotion—a way to leave a legacy of service to God and humanity.

As the cathedral began to rise, it became a focal point for the city. Parisians gathered to marvel at its progress, their imaginations captured by the sheer audacity of the endeavor. The construction site was a hive of activity, filled with the sounds of chisels striking stone, hammers pounding iron, and the voices of workers shouting instructions. It was a place where the sacred and the mundane coexisted, where the lofty ideals of faith met the gritty realities of labor.

Maurice de Sully did not live to see the completion of Notre-Dame, but his vision endured, carried forward by those who shared his dream. Each successive generation of builders added their own contributions, refining and expanding upon the original design. The continuity of this effort, spanning nearly 200 years, is a testament to the power of collective vision and perseverance.

The architects and laborers who brought Notre-Dame to life were not merely craftsmen; they were innovators and dreamers who dared to imagine the impossible. They transformed limestone and timber into a monument that defied gravity and time, a structure that continues to inspire awe and wonder. Their work was not just an expression of faith; it was a declaration of humanity's boundless potential to create and aspire.

Notre-Dame's completion marked a turning point in the history of Paris and the Gothic style. It became the standard against which all other cathedrals were measured, its influence rippling across Europe and beyond. The visionaries behind its creation had not only achieved their goal; they had set a new benchmark for architectural and artistic excellence. Their legacy endures not just in the stones of Notre-Dame but in the spirit of innovation and collaboration that defined their work.

Today, as we look at Notre-Dame—scarred but still standing—we are reminded of the courage and determination of those who first dreamed it into being. Their vision was not limited to their own time; it was a gift to the future, a reminder that great achievements require not just individual brilliance but collective effort and an unwavering belief in the possible. The story of Notre-Dame is, above all, a story of visionaries—of the people who dared to imagine a world elevated by beauty, faith, and human ingenuity.

2.Challenges of Gothic Architecture

When we look at the grandeur of Notre-Dame today, it's easy to be swept away by its soaring arches, intricate stone carvings, and luminous stained-glass windows. It seems timeless, almost otherworldly—a masterpiece that defies the limitations of human hands. Yet, behind this breathtaking beauty lies a story of struggle, ingenuity, and determination. Building a Gothic cathedral like Notre-Dame was no simple task. It was an audacious undertaking that pushed the boundaries of what was architecturally possible in the 12th and 13th centuries, requiring the resolution of countless challenges along the way.

Gothic architecture was a revolutionary departure from the Romanesque style that preceded it. Where Romanesque buildings were heavy and solid, with thick walls and small windows, Gothic cathedrals sought to achieve something far more ambitious: height, light, and a sense of divine transcendence. This meant designing structures that felt almost weightless, as if they were reaching heavenward. But translating such lofty ideals into physical reality was another matter entirely.

One of the first and most significant challenges faced by the builders of Notre-Dame was the question of weight. The very elements that defined the Gothic style—its towering ceilings, expansive windows, and intricate details— posed a structural dilemma. How could a building support its own immense weight while still achieving the verticality and openness that the style demanded? Traditional techniques were insufficient; innovation was essential.

The solution came in the form of ribbed vaults. These ingenious structures allowed builders to distribute weight more evenly across the walls, reducing the pressure concentrated on any single point. By channeling the forces downward along specific lines, ribbed vaults made it possible to create higher ceilings without sacrificing stability. However, implementing this innovation was far from straightforward. The construction of ribbed vaults required precise calculations and extraordinary craftsmanship. A single misstep could cause the entire structure to collapse. This was no small risk in an era when mathematics and engineering were still developing fields, and much of the work relied on trial and error.

Even with ribbed vaults, the walls of Notre-Dame would have needed to be impossibly thick to support the weight of the structure. This would have defeated the purpose of the Gothic style, which sought to replace dark, enclosed spaces with light-filled, open ones. Enter another groundbreaking innovation: the flying buttress. These external supports extended out from the cathedral, counteracting the outward thrust of the walls and allowing them to rise higher and incorporate larger windows. The flying buttresses of Notre-Dame are among the earliest examples of this technique, and their implementation was a feat of engineering genius.

However, the introduction of flying buttresses brought its own challenges. First and foremost was the issue of aesthetics. These external supports, though functional, could have appeared clunky and out of place, disrupting the overall harmony of the design. To address this, the architects of Notre-Dame turned to decoration. The buttresses were adorned with intricate carvings and statues, transforming them into artistic elements that complemented the cathedral's beauty. These details were not mere embellishments; they were carefully considered components of a unified vision.

The process of constructing the flying buttresses was itself fraught with difficulties. They required immense quantities of stone, which had to be quarried, transported, and carved with painstaking precision. The placement of each buttress had to be meticulously calculated to ensure that it provided the necessary support without compromising the integrity of the structure. Achieving this balance was a constant challenge, one that demanded not only technical skill but also a deep understanding of the materials and forces at play.

Another major challenge was the creation of Notre-Dame's iconic stained-glass windows. These magnificent works of art are not only visually stunning but also structurally integral, as they replaced much of the stone traditionally used in walls. The sheer size of these windows was unprecedented at the time, and their construction required innovations in both glassmaking and metalwork. Artisans had to develop techniques for producing larger panes of glass in vibrant colors, as well as for crafting the intricate lead frameworks that held them together. Each window was a collaborative effort involving glaziers, metalworkers, and artists, all working in harmony to bring the designs to life.

The challenges of Gothic architecture were not limited to technical considerations; they also extended to the human element. Building Notre-Dame required an army of laborers, including stonecutters, masons, carpenters, and blacksmiths. Coordinating such a diverse workforce was a monumental task, especially over the course of a project that spanned nearly two centuries. Workers faced grueling conditions, often laboring in harsh weather and under dangerous circumstances. Injuries were common, and the physical toll was immense. Yet, despite these hardships, there was a shared sense of purpose that drove them forward—a belief that they were part of something greater than themselves.

The construction of Notre-Dame also posed logistical challenges. The cathedral's location on the Île de la Cité, surrounded by the Seine, made transportation of materials particularly difficult. Stone for the walls had to be quarried miles away and transported by boat, a process that was time-consuming and expensive. Timber for the roof, which required massive quantities of oak, presented another logistical hurdle. Entire forests were felled to supply the wood, and the task of transporting and shaping it required incredible effort and coordination.

Weather, too, was an ever-present challenge. Rain could turn the construction site into a muddy quagmire, while cold winters made it difficult to work with stone and mortar. Each season brought its own obstacles, yet the builders persevered, driven by the vision of what Notre-Dame could become.

Despite the immense difficulties, the challenges of Gothic architecture were also opportunities for innovation and creativity. The solutions devised by the builders of Notre-Dame not only shaped the cathedral itself but also influenced the development of architecture for centuries to come. The techniques pioneered in its construction were adopted and refined by other Gothic cathedrals across Europe, from Chartres to Canterbury, leaving an indelible mark on the history of architecture.

In the end, the challenges faced by the visionaries and builders of Notre-Dame were not just technical but deeply human. They required imagination, collaboration, and an unwavering commitment to a shared goal. The result was a structure that seemed to defy gravity and time, a testament to what can be achieved when ambition meets ingenuity.

Today, as we marvel at Notre-Dame's beauty, it is easy to forget the struggles that made it possible. But behind every soaring arch and luminous window lies a story of determination and resilience—a reminder that greatness is never achieved without overcoming great challenges.

3.Building a Masterpiece: The Construction Timeline

The construction of Notre-Dame de Paris is a tale of ambition, innovation, and perseverance spanning nearly two centuries. It was a project of such monumental scale and complexity that its completion required not only the ingenuity of architects and craftsmen but also the unwavering commitment of generations of workers. This timeline is more than a sequence of dates and milestones—it is the story of a masterpiece coming to life, shaped by the challenges and triumphs of its creators.

The first stone of Notre-Dame was laid in 1163 under the watchful eye of Maurice de Sully, Bishop of Paris. The decision to build the cathedral was born out of necessity and aspiration. The existing church of Saint-Étienne, though significant in its own right, was deemed insufficient for the growing city of Paris and the rising prominence of the Catholic Church. Maurice de Sully envisioned a cathedral that would not only reflect the glory of God but also assert the spiritual and political importance of Paris as a center of power in medieval Europe.

Construction began with the choir, the sacred heart of the cathedral where the clergy would lead the congregation in worship. This phase, completed around 1177, set the tone for the entire project. The choir's soaring arches and ribbed vaults showcased the groundbreaking Gothic style, which allowed for greater height and light, contrasting sharply with the heavy, dim interiors of earlier Romanesque churches. It was here that the first innovations of Notre-Dame came to life, blending faith and engineering in unprecedented ways.

By the early 1180s, attention turned to the nave, the central space where the faithful would gather. The nave was designed to accommodate the growing population of Paris, which had become one of the most important cities in Europe. This phase required meticulous planning and extraordinary craftsmanship. The construction of the nave's towering walls and massive columns was a painstaking process, each stone carefully cut and placed to ensure stability. The installation of the ribbed vaults above the nave was a particularly challenging feat, requiring precise calculations and daring ingenuity.

As the 13th century dawned, work on the western facade began, a phase that would leave an indelible mark on the cathedral's identity. The twin towers that dominate the facade today were a marvel of Gothic architecture, embodying both strength and grace. Their construction was a laborious process, involving the coordination of countless artisans and laborers. The facade's intricate carvings and statues, depicting biblical scenes and saints, were not merely decorative but served as a form of storytelling, bringing the teachings of the Church to life for an audience that was largely illiterate.

The construction of the western facade also introduced one of Notre-Dame's most iconic features: its rose windows. These massive circular stained-glass masterpieces are among the finest examples of medieval art, their vibrant colors and intricate designs capturing the divine light in ways that still inspire awe today. The rose windows were a collaborative effort, combining the skills of glaziers, metalworkers, and artists to create a symphony of light and color that transformed the cathedral's interior.

Despite these triumphs, the construction of Notre-Dame was far from smooth. The project faced numerous setbacks, from funding shortages to political upheaval. The reigns of multiple kings came and went, each leaving their mark on the cathedral in some way. The work paused and resumed countless times, reflecting the challenges of sustaining such a massive endeavor over decades. Yet, through it all, the builders persevered, driven by a shared vision of creating something that would endure for centuries.

By the mid-13th century, much of the main structure of Notre-Dame was complete, but the work was far from over. The following decades saw the addition of key features that defined the cathedral's character. The flying buttresses, introduced during the early stages of construction, were expanded and refined to provide additional support for the soaring walls and windows. These architectural marvels not only ensured the cathedral's stability but also became a defining element of its aesthetic, their elegant arcs blending functionality with beauty.

The spire, another iconic feature of Notre-Dame, was added in the 13th century. Rising high above the cathedral, it was a symbolic gesture, pointing heavenward and reinforcing the connection between the earthly and the divine. Constructed from timber and covered in lead, the spire was both a technical achievement and a spiritual statement, a testament to the ambition of the builders and the faith that inspired them.

The construction of Notre-Dame officially concluded in the early 14th century, but in truth, the cathedral was never truly finished. Over the centuries, it underwent numerous modifications and restorations, reflecting the changing tastes, needs, and challenges of each era. The spire, for example, was rebuilt in the 19th century after being removed during the French Revolution, while the rose windows were meticulously restored following damage sustained during various conflicts.

Throughout its construction and beyond, Notre-Dame was a living monument, shaped not only by its architects and builders but also by the countless individuals who contributed to its upkeep and preservation. Each generation left its mark, adding to the cathedral's story and ensuring its survival for those who came after.

The timeline of Notre-Dame's construction is a testament to human ingenuity and perseverance. It is a story of individuals working together to create something greater than themselves, driven by faith, creativity, and a desire to leave a lasting legacy. The result is a masterpiece that has stood the test of time, inspiring awe and wonder in all who behold it.

Today, as we look back on the construction of Notre-Dame, it is impossible not to marvel at the vision and determination that brought it to life. Each phase of its construction represents a chapter in the story of human achievement, a reminder of what we can accomplish when we dare to dream big and work together to turn those dreams into reality.

4.The Cathedral's Role in Medieval Society

Chapter 2: A Witness to History : Revolutions, Wars, and Restorations

1.Notre-Dame During the French Revolution

In the bustling streets of medieval Paris, life unfolded in a whirlwind of commerce, faith, and community. At the heart of it all stood Notre-Dame de Paris, not just as an architectural wonder but as a vibrant and integral part of everyday life. In an era defined by religious devotion and a tightly woven social fabric, the cathedral was far more than a place of worship. It was the center of spiritual life, a hub of community activity, and a symbol of the city's identity, embodying the hopes and aspirations of a society striving to balance earthly concerns with heavenly ideals.

For the people of medieval Paris, religion was not a private matter; it was the foundation of their worldview, shaping every aspect of life from birth to death. Notre-Dame served as the spiritual anchor of the city, a place where the sacred intersected with the mundane. Its towering presence reminded Parisians of the divine, inspiring both awe and reverence. The cathedral's bells marked the passage of time, not just in hours but in the rhythm of daily life, calling the faithful to prayer and signaling moments of collective celebration or mourning.

The rituals conducted within Notre-Dame's walls were central to the lives of the city's inhabitants. Baptisms, marriages, and funerals—the milestones of life—were sanctified here, linking individuals and families to the greater narrative of their faith. The cathedral also played a key role in the liturgical calendar, hosting elaborate ceremonies for holy days such as Easter and Christmas. These events were grand spectacles, combining music, art, and drama to convey the mysteries of faith to a largely illiterate population. For many, the rituals at Notre-Dame were not just acts of devotion but deeply emotional experiences, moments of connection with the divine.

But Notre-Dame's role extended beyond the spiritual realm. In medieval society, the cathedral was a meeting place where the boundaries between the sacred and secular often blurred. The plaza in front of Notre-Dame was a lively gathering spot, teeming with merchants, entertainers, and townsfolk going about their business. Markets were often held here, and the steps of the cathedral served as an impromptu stage for public announcements, debates, and even performances. It was a space where all walks of life converged, reflecting the vibrant diversity of the city.

The cathedral also played an important role in education and knowledge. Attached to Notre-Dame was a school that would later evolve into the

University of Paris, one of the most prestigious centers of learning in the medieval world. Clergy associated with the cathedral were often scholars and teachers, tasked with not only preserving religious texts but also advancing knowledge in fields such as philosophy, astronomy, and medicine. For students and intellectuals, Notre-Dame was both a spiritual sanctuary and a beacon of enlightenment, a place where faith and reason coexisted.

Justice, too, was dispensed under the shadow of Notre-Dame. The cathedral was often the site of public trials and proclamations, reinforcing its position as a cornerstone of civic life. Its authority extended beyond the spiritual, serving as a moral arbiter in a society deeply intertwined with the Church. Those accused of crimes sometimes sought sanctuary within its walls, invoking the ancient right of asylum. This practice underscored the cathedral's role as a protector of the vulnerable, even as it reflected the complexities of medieval law and power.

For the city's poor and marginalized, Notre-Dame was a place of refuge and charity. The Church played a vital role in caring for the needy, distributing alms and providing shelter to those without homes. Notre-Dame's clergy were tasked with administering this aid, embodying the Church's mission to serve the less fortunate. The cathedral thus became a symbol of hope for those on the fringes of society, a tangible representation of compassion and mercy.

Art and culture also flourished around Notre-Dame, fueled by its status as a patron of creativity. The cathedral itself was a canvas for the finest artisans of the age, from sculptors and stonemasons to painters and musicians. Its soaring architecture and intricate details reflected not only the glory of God but also the skill and imagination of its creators. Music, in particular, thrived within Notre-Dame's walls. The cathedral was a center for the development of polyphony, a groundbreaking style of composition that laid the foundation for much of Western music. The resonant acoustics of its vast interior provided the perfect setting for these innovations, filling the space with sounds that seemed to echo the heavens.

Notre-Dame's influence extended beyond Paris, shaping the identity of France itself. As the seat of the Archbishop of Paris, the cathedral was a focal point for national events, from the coronation of kings to the declaration of peace treaties. Its prominence symbolized the unity of Church and state, a cornerstone of medieval governance. In times of crisis, such as wars or plagues, Notre-Dame served as a rallying point, where prayers were offered, and processions held to seek divine intervention. For the people of France, the cathedral was not just a local treasure but a symbol of their collective strength and resilience.

Despite its grandeur, Notre-Dame was not immune to the challenges of the age. The medieval period was marked by political intrigue, social upheaval, and periodic outbreaks of disease. The cathedral bore witness to these trials, standing as a steadfast presence amid uncertainty. Its construction, which spanned nearly 200 years, was itself a reflection of the resilience and determination of the society that built it. Each generation contributed to its completion, investing not just labor but a sense of identity and purpose.

In many ways, Notre-Dame was a mirror of medieval society, reflecting its complexities, contradictions, and aspirations. It was a place where faith met commerce, where learning coexisted with tradition, and where the sacred and secular intertwined. For the people of Paris, the cathedral was not just a building but a living entity, a space that shaped and was shaped by the community it served.

Today, as we marvel at Notre-Dame's beauty and history, it is worth remembering its origins as a cornerstone of medieval life. The cathedral was more than monument to faith; it was a testament to the human spirit, a place where the everyday and the eternal came together in a harmonious whole. In its towering arches and luminous windows, we can still glimpse the hopes and dreams of the people who built it—a reminder of the enduring legacy of a society that sought to bring heaven to earth.

2. The Coronation of Napoleon Bonaparte

By the time of the French Revolution, Notre-Dame de Paris had already stood for over six centuries, its towering spires and intricate stonework a testament to the ingenuity and faith of the medieval builders who had created it. Yet, in the late 18th century, this grand cathedral found itself in the crosshairs of a revolution that sought to upend the very institutions it had long symbolized. The Revolution's ideals of liberty, equality, and fraternity were not just a rejection of monarchy but also a challenge to the authority of the Catholic Church, with Notre-Dame caught in the tumultuous storm.

The Revolution began in 1789 as a movement against the entrenched privileges of the monarchy and the Church, both of which were seen as complicit in perpetuating inequality. For centuries, Notre-Dame had been a beacon of Catholic power, hosting grand ceremonies, royal coronations, and the solemn gatherings of the clergy. To the revolutionaries, it represented an oppressive past, a symbol of a system they sought to dismantle. Its soaring arches and intricate statues, once admired as manifestations of divine glory, became targets for those eager to erase the old order.

The cathedral's ordeal began with its confiscation by the revolutionary government. Notre-Dame, like many other church properties, was declared national property in 1790, stripping it of its connection to the Catholic Church. At first, the changes were superficial. Religious services continued, albeit under increasing scrutiny. However, as the Revolution radicalized and the Reign of Terror gripped France, the cathedral's fate grew precarious.

In 1793, the revolutionary fervor reached its peak. The Cult of Reason, a secular ideology promoting Enlightenment values over religious dogma, was established, and Notre-Dame was repurposed as a "Temple of Reason." The transformation was both symbolic and practical. Statues of saints were removed or desecrated, replaced with allegorical figures representing Liberty and Reason. The grand altar, once the focal point of Catholic worship, was stripped of its sacred artifacts and used for civic ceremonies. Even the Virgin Mary, long venerated as a figure of compassion and hope, was replaced with an image of Liberty.

The desecration of Notre-Dame went beyond its physical structure. The cathedral's bells, which had rung out over Paris for centuries, calling the faithful to prayer and marking significant moments in the city's history, were silenced. Most were melted down to create cannons for the revolutionary army, their booming chimes transformed into instruments of war. The massive bronze statues of the apostles, which adorned the spire, were removed and destroyed. Only a few of the cathedral's treasures, such as the Crown of Thorns, were saved, thanks to the efforts of brave individuals who risked their lives to protect these relics from destruction.

One of the most dramatic acts of desecration occurred in 1793 when the statues of the biblical kings on the cathedral's facade were decapitated by a revolutionary mob. Mistaken for representations of the French monarchy, these statues became unintended victims of revolutionary zeal. Their headless bodies remained in place for decades, a haunting reminder of the chaos and violence of the Revolution. The severed heads, thought lost for centuries, were only rediscovered in the 20th century, buried nearby—a poignant testament to the layers of history buried within Notre-Dame's stones.

Inside the cathedral, the damage was equally profound. The nave, once filled with the reverent sounds of prayer and hymn, became a stage for revolutionary festivals and gatherings. The grandeur of Notre-Dame was repurposed to glorify the new order, its sacred space converted into a theater of politics. Yet, even as the revolutionaries sought to erase its religious significance, the cathedral's soaring architecture and luminous windows seemed to resist. The very structure of Notre-Dame, designed to inspire awe and elevate the spirit, could not be fully subdued by the fervor of the moment.

As the Reign of Terror gave way to the more moderate Directory in 1795, the cathedral's fortunes began to shift. Religious practices were cautiously reinstated, and Notre-Dame was returned to the Catholic Church, though it remained under strict state control. However, the damage inflicted during the Revolution was not easily undone. The once-majestic cathedral stood battered and scarred, a shadow of its former self.

Notre-Dame's story during the French Revolution is not just one of destruction but also of resilience. Despite the physical and symbolic assaults it endured, the cathedral survived, its foundations intact. Its endurance was a testament to the strength of its construction and the enduring power of its design, which continued to inspire even in its darkest days. For the people of Paris, Notre-Dame remained a presence, a reminder of their city's history and identity.

The Revolution left an indelible mark on Notre-Dame, but it also set the stage for its eventual restoration. In the decades that followed, the cathedral became a symbol of renewal and hope, its scars a reminder of the trials it had endured. The work of preserving and restoring Notre-Dame, most notably under the guidance of the 19th-century architect Eugène Viollet-le-Duc, was not just an act of architectural repair but also a reclamation of its significance as a cultural and spiritual icon.

Today, as we look at Notre-Dame, it is impossible not to think of its turbulent journey through the French Revolution. The cathedral's survival through this period is a testament to its resilience and its ability to adapt to the changing tides of history. Its stones bear witness to the passions, conflicts, and ideals of the time, standing as a silent reminder of the complexity of human progress. The story of Notre-Dame during the Revolution is not just a chapter in its history but a reflection of the broader struggles and triumphs of humanity itself.

3.Surviving Two World Wars

Notre-Dame de Paris, a sentinel of faith and art, bore witness to two of the most tumultuous events in modern history: World War I and World War II. In both conflicts, the cathedral stood at the crossroads of destruction and endurance, a silent observer to the chaos that engulfed Paris and the world. Despite the devastation that surrounded it, Notre-Dame emerged largely unscathed, its survival a testament to both its enduring strength and the reverence it commanded, even in times of war.

When World War I erupted in 1914, Paris found itself on the frontlines of a new and terrifying kind of warfare. The city braced for bombardment as the German army advanced, and Notre-Dame, like many of France's cultural treasures, faced the threat of destruction. While the cathedral was never directly targeted, it remained under constant danger as air raids and artillery strikes became a regular part of life in Paris.

During these tense years, Notre-Dame served as both a sanctuary and a symbol. For Parisians, it was a place to seek solace amid the uncertainty of war. Its vast nave, illuminated by the colors of its stained-glass windows, offered a quiet refuge where people could pray, reflect, or simply escape the harsh realities of the outside world. The cathedral's bells, silenced early in the war to avoid drawing attention from enemy aircraft, became a poignant reminder of the city's resilience. Though muted, they remained a symbol of hope, a promise that life would continue even in the darkest of times.

As the war progressed, Notre-Dame took on an even greater role in the collective spirit of the nation. Religious services held within its walls became moments of unity, drawing people from all walks of life to gather and find strength in their shared faith and heritage. These ceremonies, often attended by soldiers and their families, provided a sense of continuity and purpose. They reminded the people of France that their culture and identity were worth preserving, even as the world around them seemed to crumble.

The armistice of 1918 brought relief and celebration, and Notre-Dame played a central role in the city's expressions of gratitude and joy. On November 11, the cathedral's bells rang out for the first time in years, their peals echoing through the streets of Paris. The sound was met with cheers and tears, a collective outpouring of emotion that symbolized the end of the conflict and the resilience of the city and its people. In the years that followed, Notre-Dame hosted countless memorial services for those lost in the war, its stones absorbing the grief and gratitude of a nation rebuilding itself.

Two decades later, Paris faced an even greater challenge as World War II descended upon Europe. In 1940, the German army marched into the city, and Paris fell under Nazi occupation. The city's landmarks, including Notre-Dame, were suddenly at the mercy of a regime known for looting and destroying cultural heritage. The cathedral's fate hung in the balance, its future uncertain in a city now ruled by foreign forces.

Despite the occupation, Notre-Dame retained its place as a symbol of French identity and resistance. The cathedral remained open for religious services, which became acts of quiet defiance against the Nazi regime. Parisians gathered within its walls to pray for liberation, their faith and hope unbroken even as their city lay under the shadow of tyranny. The cathedral's enduring presence provided a sense of continuity and stability in a time of profound upheaval.

One of the most remarkable moments in Notre-Dame's wartime history came in 1944, during the liberation of Paris. As Allied forces approached the city, the German military commander, General Dietrich von Choltitz, was ordered by Adolf Hitler to destroy Paris's landmarks, including Notre-Dame, rather than allow them to fall into Allied hands. Yet, in an extraordinary act of defiance, von Choltitz refused to carry out the order. His decision spared the cathedral, along with much of the city's architectural heritage, from destruction.

On August 26, 1944, just days after Paris was freed from Nazi control, a triumphant mass was held in Notre-Dame to celebrate the city's liberation. The service, attended by General Charles de Gaulle and thousands of Parisians, was a moment of profound unity and joy. The sound of the cathedral's bells, ringing freely once more, symbolized not just the end of the occupation but the enduring spirit of Paris and its people. Images of the event, showing de Gaulle walking solemnly through the nave, became iconic, capturing the resilience and triumph of a city that had endured so much.

In the aftermath of World War II, Notre-Dame continued to serve as a place of remembrance and reflection. Memorial services for the victims of the Holocaust and the fallen soldiers of France were held within its walls, as the cathedral became a space for healing and reconciliation. Its survival during the war, untouched by bombs or fire, was seen by many as a miracle, a sign of its sacredness and the profound respect it commanded.

The legacy of Notre-Dame's survival through two world wars is a story of resilience, not just of stone and glass, but of the human spirit. The cathedral stood as a beacon of hope, a reminder that even in the face of unimaginable destruction, there are things that endure—symbols of faith, culture, and identity that no war can destroy. Its continued presence offered solace to those who had lost so much and inspiration to those rebuilding their lives.

Today, as we look at Notre-Dame, it is impossible not to think of the challenges it has faced and overcome. From the air raids of World War I to the occupation of World War II, the cathedral has borne witness to some of the darkest moments in modern history. Yet, through it all, it has remained a steadfast symbol of resilience and hope, a reminder of the enduring power of faith and the strength of a people united in the face of adversity.

Notre-Dame's survival through two world wars is not just a testament to its architectural strength but to its place in the hearts of those who cherish it. It is a reminder that even in the most trying times, there are things worth preserving—symbols of beauty, faith, and humanity that connect us to our past and inspire us to build a better future.

4. Victor Hugo and the Cathedral's Revival

By the early 19th century, Notre-Dame de Paris was a shadow of its former self. Once a symbol of medieval grandeur, the cathedral had fallen into disrepair, its stone walls weathered by centuries and its intricate sculptures defaced during the tumultuous years of the French Revolution. Statues were decapitated, treasures looted, and the once-majestic interior left neglected. It was no longer a proud beacon of faith and culture but a crumbling relic, overshadowed by the rapidly modernizing city around it.

In the eyes of many, Notre-Dame's fate seemed sealed. There was talk of demolishing the cathedral entirely, its ruins to be replaced by something more "modern" and "useful." Yet, this impending doom would be forestalled, thanks to one man's vision: Victor Hugo.

Hugo, already an acclaimed writer by the 1830s, was deeply troubled by the disregard for France's medieval heritage. For him, Notre-Dame was not merely an architectural landmark; it was a cornerstone of French identity, a testament to the creativity and craftsmanship of a bygone era. He lamented the neglect of such treasures, believing that the destruction of historic monuments severed the connection between the past and future. In his view, Notre-Dame was a masterpiece of human achievement, and its decline reflected a dangerous apathy toward cultural preservation.

It was this passion that led Hugo to pen his seminal novel, *Notre-Dame de Paris*, published in 1831 and known to English readers as *The Hunchback of Notre-Dame*. The novel was far more than a romantic tale of Quasimodo, the kind-hearted bell ringer, and Esmeralda, the tragic gypsy girl. It was a love letter to the cathedral itself, a vivid portrayal of its beauty, complexity, and significance.

Hugo's descriptions of Notre-Dame brought the cathedral to life in a way that transcended mere words. He painted it as a living, breathing entity—an enduring witness to centuries of Parisian history. Through his prose, readers could feel the cool stone beneath their hands, hear the resonant toll of the bells, and marvel at the kaleidoscope of light streaming through its stained-glass windows. Hugo captured not just the physical structure but the soul of Notre-Dame, presenting it as a character in its own right.

The novel's impact was immediate and profound. It captured the imagination of the French public, many of whom had never given much thought to the cathedral's decline. For the first time in decades, Notre-Dame became a topic of national conversation. Readers were enthralled by Hugo's vivid portrayal of the cathedral, and they began to see it not as a decaying relic but as a vital part of their cultural heritage. The novel ignited a wave of nostalgia and pride, sparking a newfound appreciation for France's medieval past.

Hugo's influence extended beyond the literary world. The popularity of *Notre-Dame de Paris* inspired a broader cultural movement to preserve historic monuments, leading to the establishment of organizations dedicated to their restoration. In 1837, just a few years after the novel's publication, King Louis-Philippe authorized a major restoration project for Notre-Dame, a decision directly influenced by the public outcry that Hugo's work had stirred.

The restoration, overseen by architect Eugène Viollet-le-Duc, was as ambitious as it was meticulous. Viollet-le-Duc shared Hugo's reverence for the cathedral and approached the project with a deep sense of responsibility. His goal was not merely to repair the damage but to restore Notre-Dame to its original grandeur, respecting its medieval origins while incorporating his own artistic vision.

Under Viollet-le-Duc's guidance, Notre-Dame underwent a dramatic transformation. Missing or damaged statues were replaced, including the famous chimeras and gargoyles that now grace the cathedral's exterior. The spire, which had been removed after the Revolution, was rebuilt, rising majestically above the skyline of Paris. The interior was painstakingly restored, with attention given to every detail, from the carvings on the choir stalls to the vibrant hues of the stained-glass windows.

The restoration was not without controversy. Critics accused Viollet-le-Duc of taking liberties with the cathedral's design, arguing that some of his additions, such as the gargoyles, were more reflective of his own imagination than of historical accuracy. Yet, despite these debates, the project succeeded in reviving Notre-Dame's status as a symbol of French heritage. By the time the restoration was completed in the mid-19th century, the cathedral had reclaimed its place as one of Paris's most iconic landmarks.

Victor Hugo, though not directly involved in the restoration, watched its progress with pride. His novel had achieved its purpose, awakening a sense of responsibility toward preserving France's architectural legacy. In the years that followed, Notre-Dame became a magnet for tourists, scholars, and artists, its renewed grandeur inspiring countless works of art and literature.

The revival of Notre-Dame also had a profound impact on Hugo himself. The success of *Notre-Dame de Paris* solidified his reputation as one of France's greatest writers, and his advocacy for cultural preservation became a defining aspect of his career. Hugo's vision extended beyond the cathedral; he championed the protection of historic sites across France, believing that these monuments were vital to the nation's identity and collective memory.

Today, it is impossible to separate the story of Notre-Dame from that of Victor Hugo. His novel not only saved the cathedral from destruction but also ensured its place in the hearts of millions around the world. Notre-Dame stands as a testament to the power of storytelling, a reminder that art and literature can shape the course of history.

Hugo's legacy endures in every stone of Notre-Dame, in every curve of its arches and every note of its bells. His passion for the cathedral reminds us that our shared heritage is worth preserving, not just for its beauty but for the stories it tells and the connections it fosters across generations. Through his words, Hugo gave Notre-Dame a voice, one that continues to resonate across the centuries.

As visitors stand beneath the cathedral's soaring ceilings or gaze up at its intricate facade, they are witnessing not just an architectural marvel but the culmination of a revival sparked by a single man's love for a crumbling monument. Victor Hugo's words breathed new life into Notre-Dame, ensuring that it would remain a symbol of resilience, creativity, and the enduring power of human imagination.

Chapter 3: Secrets of the Stone : Hidden Symbols and Architectural Mysteries

1.Decoding the Gargoyles: Guardians or Decorations?

Perched high upon the edges of Notre-Dame de Paris, the gargoyles peer down with menacing glares and grotesque grins. Their forms are both fascinating and unsettling—part creature, part fantasy. These stone figures have captured the imaginations of countless visitors, inspiring myths, stories, and interpretations over the centuries. But what purpose do they truly serve? Are they mere decorations, whimsical flights of the stonemason's imagination? Or do they have a deeper, perhaps even mystical, significance?

The gargoyles of Notre-Dame are far more than ornamental flourishes. They are functional, symbolic, and enigmatic—elements that reflect the complexities of Gothic architecture and the cultural mindsets of the medieval world. To understand their role, we must explore their history, their meanings, and the enduring mystery they embody.

The most practical explanation for gargoyles lies in their original function as waterspouts. The word "gargoyle" itself is derived from the Old French *gargouille*, meaning "throat" or "gullet," a reference to their role in directing rainwater away from the cathedral's walls. Medieval architects faced the challenge of preventing water damage to their towering structures, and the solution they devised was both ingenious and artistic. By carving elaborate spouts that jutted out from the building, they could ensure that rainwater drained far from the stone facade, protecting it from erosion.

But if gargoyles were purely functional, why were they sculpted into such fantastical forms? Here lies the deeper, symbolic layer of their existence. For the medieval mind, gargoyles were not just utilitarian; they were protectors. They were imagined as guardians of the sacred, keeping evil spirits and demonic forces at bay. Their grotesque appearances served a dual purpose: they were both frightening to malevolent entities and awe-inspiring to those who stood in the cathedral's shadow. To the faithful, these monstrous figures were a reassurance that the sacred space of Notre-Dame was shielded by forces greater than themselves.

The symbolism of gargoyles draws heavily from medieval Christian cosmology, which often merged religious teachings with folklore and superstition. In a world where fear of the unknown was a constant companion, gargoyles were seen as intermediaries between the earthly and the divine. Their grotesque forms represented the chaos and danger of the world outside the cathedral, a stark contrast to the sanctuary and order within. By placing these creatures on the exterior, medieval architects created a powerful visual metaphor: the Church was a refuge from the darkness and sin that lurked beyond its walls.

The gargoyles also served as moral reminders. Their contorted faces and grotesque forms were a visual representation of the consequences of sin and the peril of straying from the path of righteousness. In this way, they acted as silent preachers, conveying lessons through their very presence. Their grotesqueness was not meant to horrify but to instruct, reinforcing the moral and spiritual values of the time.

Yet, not all the figures adorning Notre-Dame are true gargoyles. Many of the stone creatures that visitors find so captivating are technically chimeras— sculptures without the water-spouting function. These figures, which include winged beasts, horned demons, and even hybrid creatures, were added during the 19th-century restoration led by Eugène Viollet-le-Duc. Unlike their medieval predecessors, these chimeras were created purely for aesthetic and symbolic purposes, reflecting the Gothic Revival's romantic fascination with the macabre and the mystical.

Viollet-le-Duc's most famous addition is the Stryga, often referred to as "The Spitting Gargoyle." This contemplative, horned figure rests its chin on clawed hands, gazing out over the city of Paris. The Stryga has become one of Notre-Dame's most iconic figures, embodying the sense of mystery and melancholy often associated with the cathedral. Though it lacks the functional purpose of the original gargoyles, it captures the spirit of their role as silent observers and guardians of the sacred.

The duality of Notre-Dame's gargoyles—as both protectors and decorations—has fueled countless interpretations and stories. Some see them as vestiges of pagan influences, remnants of a time when ancient spirits were invoked to guard sacred spaces. Others view them as purely artistic expressions, a testament to the creative freedom afforded to medieval stonemasons. The truth likely lies somewhere in between. Gargoyles were both practical and symbolic, a perfect example of how Gothic architecture merged function with meaning.

Over the centuries, the gargoyles have become more than architectural features; they have entered the realm of legend. Tales abound of these stone creatures coming to life under the light of the full moon, patrolling the cathedral's heights to fend off evil. Such stories, while fantastical, speak to the enduring power of the gargoyles to capture the imagination. They are not merely static figures but dynamic presences, imbued with a sense of life and purpose.

The gargoyles of Notre-Dame have also inspired artistic and literary works, most notably Victor Hugo's *Notre-Dame de Paris*. In Hugo's novel, the gargoyles are almost sentient, their grotesque forms reflecting the struggles and complexities of the human condition. Quasimodo, the novel's hunchbacked protagonist, is often likened to the gargoyles—an outcast who, despite his appearance, possesses profound inner beauty and loyalty. Through Hugo's lens, the gargoyles become symbols of resilience and hidden strength, mirroring the cathedral itself.

Today, as visitors gaze up at Notre-Dame's gargoyles, they are often struck by their timelessness. Despite centuries of weathering, these stone sentinels remain as haunting and enigmatic as ever. Their faces, frozen in expressions of menace or contemplation, invite questions that may never be fully answered. What did their creators imagine as they carved these figures? Did they see them as protectors, warnings, or something else entirely? Each gargoyle seems to hold its own story, a fragment of a mystery that has endured for centuries.

As guardians or decorations, the gargoyles of Notre-Dame fulfill a role that transcends their original purpose. They connect the past to the present, embodying the fears, hopes, and creativity of the people who built and preserved the cathedral. They remind us that architecture is not just about buildings but about the meanings and emotions we project onto them. In the end, the gargoyles are not merely features of Notre-Dame—they are part of its soul, a testament to the enduring power of human imagination.

2. The Mystical Labyrinth of the Cathedral

Beneath the grandeur of Notre-Dame's vaulted ceilings and towering spires lies a lesser-known but equally captivating feature: the mystical labyrinth. Though its traces have faded with time, this intricate design once graced the floor of the cathedral, weaving a path of mystery and symbolism that has fascinated historians, theologians, and seekers for centuries. A labyrinth is not a maze in the conventional sense; there are no dead ends or wrong turns. Instead, it is a single winding path, often seen as a metaphor for the spiritual journey—a meditative walk toward enlightenment or divine connection.

The labyrinth of Notre-Dame, like others found in medieval cathedrals across Europe, was more than a decorative element. It was a symbolic and functional feature, deeply rooted in the religious and cultural practices of its time. While the precise origins and purpose of Notre-Dame's labyrinth remain subjects of speculation, its existence speaks to the profound intersection of faith, art, and mysticism that defined Gothic architecture.

Medieval Christians often viewed life as a pilgrimage—a journey fraught with challenges and temptations but ultimately leading to salvation. For those who could not embark on the physically and financially demanding pilgrimages to sacred sites such as Jerusalem or Santiago de Compostela, labyrinths provided a symbolic alternative. Walking the labyrinth was seen as a devotional act, a way to simulate the pilgrimage experience and draw closer to God. The path, winding yet continuous, represented the complexities of the spiritual journey, where every step brought the pilgrim closer to the divine.

The labyrinth in Notre-Dame was likely a circular or octagonal design, mirroring the style found in other great cathedrals, such as Chartres. Its placement within the nave—where the congregation gathered—ensured that it was accessible to all. The design itself would have been a marvel of geometry and artistry, its intricate patterns forming a harmonious union with the soaring architecture above. To medieval eyes, this symmetry was no coincidence; it was a reflection of the divine order, a reminder that God's presence could be found in the structure of the universe.

Walking the labyrinth was a deeply personal experience, yet it was also communal. Pilgrims and worshippers shared the same path, their steps overlapping as they moved in silence or prayer. The act was both physical and spiritual, a way to engage the body and mind in an act of devotion. The winding path allowed for reflection and introspection, inviting the walker to leave behind worldly concerns and focus on the divine. At the center of the labyrinth was often a small cross or sacred symbol, marking the culmination of the journey and the moment of connection with God.

Beyond its role in religious practice, the labyrinth also carried layers of symbolic meaning. In medieval thought, it represented the harmony of creation, the balance between chaos and order. The labyrinth's spiraling patterns echoed natural forms, from the whorls of a seashell to the orbits of celestial bodies. This connection to the natural world reinforced the belief that all of creation was interconnected, a reflection of divine wisdom.

However, the labyrinth was not without its mysteries. For some, it carried connotations of the mystical and the esoteric, a hidden knowledge accessible only to those who understood its secrets. The very act of walking the labyrinth could be seen as a form of initiation, a journey into the unknown and back again. This duality—accessible yet enigmatic—added to its allure, making it a focal point for both devotion and speculation.

Over time, the labyrinth of Notre-Dame faded into obscurity, its physical traces lost during renovations and changes to the cathedral's interior. Yet, its legacy endures, preserved in historical records and the imaginations of those who continue to explore its mysteries. For modern visitors, the labyrinth represents a forgotten chapter in Notre-Dame's history, a reminder of the profound spirituality and artistic vision that shaped the cathedral.

The symbolism of the labyrinth remains relevant today, offering timeless lessons about the nature of life and faith. Like the pilgrims of old, we find ourselves on winding paths, facing uncertainty and challenges as we seek meaning and purpose. The labyrinth teaches us that the journey is as important as the destination, that progress is not always linear, and that every step, no matter how small, brings us closer to understanding.

Notre-Dame's labyrinth also speaks to the enduring power of Gothic architecture to engage the senses and the soul. It is a testament to the creativity and vision of the medieval builders who sought to create spaces that not only inspired awe but also invited introspection and connection. In their hands, stone and mortar became vessels of meaning, capable of conveying truths that transcend time and culture.

While the labyrinth of Notre-Dame may no longer exist in its original form, its spirit endures in the cathedral itself. The winding staircases, the interplay of light and shadow, and the intricate carvings all echo the themes of the labyrinth—a journey inward and upward, toward a deeper understanding of the divine. For those who visit Notre-Dame, the labyrinth remains a hidden presence, a reminder of the mysteries that lie at the heart of this extraordinary place.

In the end, the labyrinth of Notre-Dame is more than a historical curiosity; it is a symbol of the human quest for meaning and connection. It invites us to walk its path, not just with our feet but with our minds and hearts, to explore the mysteries of faith, art, and existence. And though its stones may be lost, its lessons endure, etched into the very fabric of Notre-Dame, a cathedral that continues to inspire and captivate all who enter its doors.

3.Religious Symbolism in Gothic Art

Gothic cathedrals like Notre-Dame de Paris are often described as "sermons in stone." Every arch, window, sculpture, and carving within these towering structures carries meaning, speaking a visual language that was as rich and layered as the theological teachings it sought to convey. For the medieval mind, steeped in a world where faith was the cornerstone of life, the art and architecture of a cathedral were not merely decorative. They were acts of devotion, vessels of divine truth, and a means of communicating religious ideals to a largely illiterate population. Notre-Dame, one of the greatest achievements of Gothic art, exemplifies the profound use of religious symbolism to inspire awe, educate, and connect humanity with the divine.

One of the most striking elements of Notre-Dame's symbolic language is its use of light. In Gothic theology, light was considered a physical manifestation of God's presence, an ethereal connection between the earthly and the divine. This belief found its ultimate expression in the cathedral's stained-glass windows. These windows, often depicting biblical stories, saints, and moments of divine revelation, were more than beautiful works of art—they were portals to the sacred. As sunlight filtered through their intricate designs, it transformed the interior of the cathedral into a space suffused with a sense of the heavenly. To step inside Notre-Dame and witness the interplay of light and color was to be reminded of the divine order that governed the universe.

The rose windows, in particular, are among the most iconic examples of this symbolism. The north rose, often associated with the Virgin Mary, and the south rose, dedicated to Christ's triumphant return, are masterpieces of Gothic design. Their circular form, representing eternity and perfection, serves as a reminder of God's infinite nature. The intricate patterns within the windows, often centered around a depiction of Christ or Mary, radiate outward, drawing the viewer's eyes toward the divine at the center. This arrangement mirrored the medieval understanding of the universe, where all creation revolved around God as its ultimate source.

The carvings and sculptures that adorn the facade and interior of Notre-Dame also teem with religious symbolism. The western facade, with its three great portals, is a prime example. Each portal tells a story through its sculptural program, inviting worshippers to contemplate profound theological truths before even stepping inside. The central portal, known as the Portal of the Last Judgment, depicts Christ enthroned as judge, flanked by angels, saints, and the resurrected dead. This vivid scene was not merely a reminder of the afterlife but a moral instruction, urging viewers to consider their actions and their ultimate fate.

To the left of the Last Judgment, the Portal of the Virgin celebrates the life and intercession of Mary, presenting her as the compassionate mother of Christ and the spiritual mother of all believers. To the right, the Portal of St. Anne honors Mary's parents and emphasizes the importance of family and lineage in the divine plan. Together, these portals formed a cohesive narrative, blending salvation, mercy, and the human connection to the divine.

The gargoyles and chimeras that perch atop Notre-Dame, though often seen as grotesque curiosities, also carry symbolic weight. Their fearsome appearances were meant to ward off evil, serving as guardians of the sacred space. At the same time, their monstrous forms reminded worshippers of the chaos and sin that lay outside the cathedral's walls. By placing these figures on the exterior, medieval architects created a stark contrast between the safety and sanctity of the Church and the dangers of the secular world.

Inside the cathedral, the narrative continues. The nave, with its soaring arches and ribbed vaults, draws the eye upward, a deliberate choice designed to lift the soul toward heaven. The verticality of the Gothic style was not just an architectural feat; it was a theological statement, reflecting the aspiration to transcend the earthly and reach the divine. Every column and arch was a reminder of the spiritual journey, guiding the faithful from the material to the immaterial.

The choir stalls and altars of Notre-Dame are equally rich in symbolism. Carvings of biblical scenes and saints served as visual sermons, illustrating the stories and virtues that formed the foundation of Christian teaching. These depictions were not random; they were carefully chosen to align with the liturgical calendar, reinforcing the themes of the Church's teachings throughout the year. For a medieval worshipper, these images provided a way to connect with scripture and the lives of the saints in a deeply personal and accessible manner.

Another key feature of Gothic religious symbolism is its focus on the interplay between humility and majesty. While the grandeur of Notre-Dame's architecture inspires awe, its details often point to the humbler aspects of faith. The depictions of ordinary people, animals, and even fantastical creatures in the carvings and decorations reflect the belief that all of creation, no matter how small or seemingly insignificant, has a place in the divine order. This inclusivity extended to the faithful themselves, reminding them that they were part of God's plan, regardless of their social status or wealth.

Notre-Dame's use of religious symbolism extends beyond its physical features to the very way it was constructed. The act of building a cathedral in the Gothic era was itself a spiritual undertaking, seen as an offering to God. The labor of the masons, sculptors, and glaziers was considered a form of prayer, each chisel strike and brushstroke imbued with devotion. This sense of purpose is evident in the meticulous craftsmanship of Notre-Dame, where even the smallest details reflect a commitment to glorifying the divine.

In the centuries since its construction, Notre-Dame's symbolism has continued to resonate, transcending its original context to speak to modern audiences. Its art and architecture remain a source of inspiration, inviting visitors to reflect on the eternal questions of faith, morality, and the human connection to the divine. The cathedral's ability to communicate these themes through its design is a testament to the power of Gothic art to transcend time and culture.

Today, as we stand in the shadow of Notre-Dame, we are reminded that its symbolism is not static but alive, evolving with each generation that gazes upon its walls. Whether one sees it as a house of worship, a masterpiece of architecture, or a cultural icon, the cathedral's art continues to fulfill its purpose: to inspire awe, provoke thought, and connect humanity to something greater than itself.

4.Forgotten Rooms and Sealed Chambers

Notre-Dame de Paris, with its soaring spires and intricate stonework, has long captivated the imagination. But beyond its visible grandeur lies a hidden world, a labyrinth of forgotten rooms and sealed chambers that remain shrouded in mystery. Over its nearly 900-year history, the cathedral has accumulated countless layers of additions, renovations, and secrets. Some of these spaces were deliberately sealed, while others simply fell out of use and were forgotten over time. These hidden areas, silent and untouched, hold clues to the lives of the people who built, worshipped in, and maintained this iconic structure.

The idea of secret rooms and chambers in Notre-Dame sparks the imagination. Were they storage spaces for treasures, hiding places during times of turmoil, or simply utilitarian areas meant to support the cathedral's daily operations? The truth is as complex as the building itself, a mixture of practicality, mystery, and historical intrigue.

One of the most enigmatic features of Notre-Dame is its expansive attic, often referred to as "the forest" due to the dense network of oak beams that supported the roof. Each beam was sourced from a single tree, and the structure required an entire forest to build. This vast, shadowy space was more than just an architectural marvel; it was also a concealed world, rarely visited except by those tasked with its upkeep. The attic was inaccessible to the general public and even to most clergy, its purpose largely utilitarian—supporting the immense weight of the lead roof. Yet, over time, it became a repository for forgotten objects: discarded tools, fragments of statues, and remnants of past renovations. It was a space frozen in time, where the past seemed to linger in the dust.

The attic's secrets came to light dramatically during the devastating fire of April 15, 2019. As the flames consumed the ancient beams, many wondered what might have been lost forever. Some speculated about hidden treasures or artifacts stored in the space. While no groundbreaking discoveries were reported, the fire renewed interest in Notre-Dame's hidden corners, prompting further exploration and study.

Beneath the cathedral lies another layer of mystery: its crypt. Unlike the attic, the crypt was deliberately designed as a space for preservation and commemoration. However, its purpose evolved over time. Originally intended to house tombs and relics, the crypt eventually became a storage area for architectural fragments and artifacts uncovered during renovations. Over the centuries, it was sealed and reopened multiple times, each excavation revealing new insights into the history of Notre-Dame and the city of Paris.

One of the most significant discoveries in the crypt occurred in the 20th century, during excavations conducted to build a modern archaeological museum beneath the square in front of the cathedral. Workers uncovered a treasure trove of Roman ruins, including remnants of ancient streets, homes, and public buildings. These findings underscored the deep history of the Île de la Cité, linking Notre-Dame not only to medieval Paris but also to its ancient roots as a Roman settlement. The crypt, now a museum, offers a glimpse into this layered history, but many areas remain unexplored, raising tantalizing questions about what else might lie beneath the cathedral.

Hidden rooms are not limited to the attic and crypt. Notre-Dame's towers, the iconic sentinels that frame its western facade, contain their own secrets. These spaces were originally designed to house the cathedral's massive bells and the mechanisms that controlled them. Over time, however, the towers became more than just bell chambers. They served as observation points, storage spaces, and, in times of conflict, defensive positions. During the French Revolution, when the cathedral was repurposed as a Temple of Reason, the towers were stripped of their religious function, but their rooms remained silent witnesses to the upheaval.

One particularly fascinating feature of the towers is the spiral staircases that wind through them. These narrow, dimly lit passages connect a series of small rooms and landings, some of which are no longer accessible to the public. These spaces were once used by bell ringers, clergy, and maintenance workers, but their original purposes have been largely forgotten. Today, they stand as echoes of a time when the cathedral was a bustling center of activity, filled with people performing the myriad tasks required to keep such a massive structure functioning.

Not all hidden spaces in Notre-Dame are ancient. During the 19th-century restoration led by Eugène Viollet-le-Duc, new rooms and passages were added, blending seamlessly with the original Gothic design. Viollet-le-Duc's restorations were both practical and visionary, ensuring that Notre-Dame could accommodate the needs of a modern congregation while preserving its historical character. Some of these additions, such as storage areas and maintenance rooms, were deliberately concealed to maintain the aesthetic integrity of the cathedral. Others, such as small chapels and private prayer rooms, were designed as intimate spaces for reflection, hidden from the hustle and bustle of the nave.

The notion of hidden rooms and sealed chambers also invites speculation about what might still be undiscovered. Could there be secret passages connecting Notre-Dame to other parts of the Île de la Cité? Historical records suggest that such tunnels were used in medieval Paris, though no definitive evidence has been found beneath the cathedral itself. Similarly, legends persist about treasure hidden within the walls of Notre-Dame, left behind by clergy or revolutionaries seeking to safeguard precious items during times of crisis. While such stories are often dismissed as fanciful, they add to the allure of the cathedral's hidden spaces.

For historians and archaeologists, the forgotten rooms of Notre-Dame are not just curiosities—they are invaluable resources for understanding the cathedral's history. Each sealed chamber and hidden corner holds clues about the lives of those who built and maintained the cathedral, the challenges they faced, and the innovations they employed. These spaces offer a tangible connection to the past, a way to walk in the footsteps of those who shaped Notre-Dame into the masterpiece it is today.

As restoration efforts continue in the wake of the 2019 fire, the hidden rooms and sealed chambers of Notre-Dame remain a source of fascination and discovery. Each new exploration brings to light forgotten aspects of the cathedral's history, deepening our understanding of its role as a living monument. These spaces, though often overlooked, are integral to Notre-Dame's story—a story of resilience, mystery, and the enduring power of human creativity.

Chapter 4: The 2019 Fire : A Tragedy in Flames

1.The Night of the Fire: How It Happened

April 15, 2019, began as an ordinary day in Paris. The streets buzzed with life, the Seine shimmered under the spring sun, and Notre-Dame de Paris stood as it had for centuries—a guardian of the city, a symbol of faith and artistry. Tourists wandered through its vast nave, marveling at the play of light through the stained-glass windows. Workers atop the scaffolding surrounding the spire continued their painstaking restoration efforts. It was a day like any other—until it wasn't.

By early evening, the tranquility of Paris was shattered. Smoke began to rise from the roof of Notre-Dame, faint at first but soon thickening into an ominous plume. The fire, which would ultimately consume the cathedral's spire and much of its roof, had started in the attic, an area known as "the forest" for its dense network of ancient oak beams. This labyrinth of wood, some of it dating back to the 12th century, was both a marvel of medieval engineering and a perfect tinderbox. Once ignited, the dry timbers fed the flames with terrifying speed, creating an inferno that would devastate one of the world's most beloved landmarks.

The exact cause of the fire remains uncertain, though investigators believe it was likely accidental. At the time, Notre-Dame was undergoing extensive restoration, a project aimed at addressing the wear and tear inflicted by centuries of weather, pollution, and neglect. Electrical equipment used in the renovations and the heat generated by the workers' tools were among the suspected culprits. Regardless of its origin, the fire spread with an unstoppable fury, fueled by the dry wood and the confined spaces of the attic.

As the flames gained strength, alarms sounded, and workers evacuated. Initially, the scale of the fire was unclear. A small fire in a building as vast as Notre-Dame might have seemed manageable, even routine. But as smoke billowed into the evening sky, it became evident that this was no ordinary emergency. The fire brigade was called, and the first responders arrived to confront a scene that seemed almost surreal.

By the time firefighters entered the cathedral, the fire had reached the spire, the iconic centerpiece of Notre-Dame's silhouette. This towering structure, a 19th-century addition by architect Eugène Viollet-le-Duc, was constructed of wood and lead. As the flames engulfed it, the spire became a fiery torch, visible from miles away. Parisians gathered on the banks of the Seine and in nearby squares, their faces illuminated by the glow of the fire. The sight of their beloved cathedral ablaze was heartbreaking. Many wept openly; others stood in stunned silence, unable to comprehend the scale of the disaster.

Inside Notre-Dame, the heat was unbearable, and the air thick with smoke. Firefighters worked tirelessly to contain the flames, knowing that the stakes were not just architectural but deeply cultural and spiritual. Their primary goal was to prevent the fire from spreading to the twin bell towers. If the flames reached the towers, the wooden structures supporting the bells could collapse, causing catastrophic damage and potentially bringing down the entire facade.

The battle was as much a logistical challenge as a physical one. The height of the fire and the complexity of the cathedral's design made it difficult to access the flames directly. Water hoses could only reach so far, and aerial support was limited by concerns about structural stability. Dropping water from aircraft, for example, risked causing further damage to the weakened roof and walls. Instead, firefighters had to ascend into the cathedral itself, navigating the treacherous environment to combat the fire from within.

Meanwhile, efforts were underway to save Notre-Dame's priceless treasures. Clergy, volunteers, and emergency responders formed human chains to carry out sacred relics, artworks, and historical artifacts. Among the items rescued was the Crown of Thorns, believed to be the very relic worn by Christ during his crucifixion. The rescue of these items provided a glimmer of hope in an otherwise devastating night, a reminder of the human spirit's capacity for courage and determination.

As the hours passed, the fire claimed more of the cathedral's structure. The collapse of the spire was a particularly gut-wrenching moment. It fell in a fiery cascade, its descent captured on live broadcasts that were watched by millions around the world. For those who loved Notre-Dame, it was as though a piece of their own history had crumbled before their eyes.

Yet, even in the midst of despair, there were signs of resilience. The stone walls of Notre-Dame, though blackened by smoke, remained standing, their Gothic arches holding firm against the heat. The great rose windows, miraculously, survived the inferno, their intricate stained glass largely intact. And perhaps most remarkably, the altar cross at the heart of the cathedral remained unscathed, gleaming defiantly amid the rubble—a symbol of hope and renewal.

By the early hours of April 16, the fire was finally under control. Exhausted firefighters emerged from the cathedral, their faces streaked with soot and their eyes heavy with emotion. They had saved Notre-Dame from complete destruction, preserving its core structure and many of its treasures. Their heroism was met with an outpouring of gratitude from Parisians and people around the globe.

The morning light revealed the full extent of the damage. The roof was gone, replaced by a gaping hole open to the sky. The spire was no more, and the once-hidden attic had been reduced to ash. Yet, Notre-Dame stood. It was battered, scarred, but still undeniably itself—a testament to the resilience of both the cathedral and the people who fought to save it.

The night of the fire marked a turning point in Notre-Dame's history. It was a moment of profound loss but also of unity and determination. The images of the burning cathedral and the efforts to save it reminded the world of the deep connection we have to our cultural heritage. Notre-Dame was not just a building; it was a part of humanity's story, a symbol of our shared history, and a beacon of hope in times of adversity.

As restoration efforts continue today, the night of the fire remains etched in the collective memory. It is a reminder of the fragility of even the most enduring monuments and the importance of coming together to preserve what we hold dear. For Parisians and people around the world, Notre-Dame's survival is a source of inspiration, a testament to the strength of community and the enduring power of human spirit.

2.Investigating the Cause: Accidents or Negligence?

In the aftermath of the devastating fire that engulfed Notre-Dame de Paris on April 15, 2019, one question loomed large in the minds of investigators, historians, and the global public: how could such a tragedy happen? A cathedral that had withstood centuries of wars, revolutions, and natural decay was suddenly consumed by flames in a matter of hours. The search for answers became an urgent priority, not only to understand what went wrong but to ensure that such a disaster could never happen again.

From the moment the fire was extinguished, the site of Notre-Dame became a crime scene. Investigators, wearing protective gear to navigate the charred remains, combed through the debris for clues. Their task was daunting. The fire had destroyed much of the evidence, reducing centuries-old oak beams, lead roofing, and other materials to ash and molten metal. Despite the challenges, investigators began piecing together a timeline of events and identifying potential causes.

One of the earliest theories pointed to the ongoing restoration work on the cathedral's roof and spire. Notre-Dame had been undergoing a significant renovation project, aimed at addressing structural issues caused by age, weather, and pollution. Scaffolding surrounded the spire, and workers used tools such as soldering irons and electrical equipment to complete their tasks. It was suspected that the fire may have started due to an accident during these restoration efforts.

The hypothesis gained traction as details emerged about the safety measures in place—or the lack thereof. Workers had been using open flames for soldering, a practice that required strict safety protocols. While initial reports suggested that fire alarms were present and functional, questions arose about how the fire was able to spread so rapidly. Some critics argued that the response to the initial alarms had been delayed, allowing the fire to take hold before firefighters were called to the scene.

The electrical systems used on the scaffolding also came under scrutiny. Wiring and lighting installed to facilitate the restoration work were examined as potential sources of ignition. Could a short circuit or an overloaded connection have sparked the blaze? While investigators found no definitive proof, the possibility remained a key focus of the inquiry.

Another area of investigation centered on the fire alarm system itself. Notre-Dame was equipped with a sophisticated alarm network, designed to detect smoke and alert security personnel. However, on the night of the fire, the system's initial alert reportedly failed to pinpoint the exact location of the flames. Security staff were dispatched to investigate, but by the time the fire was discovered in the attic, it had already spread beyond control. This delay, while brief, proved catastrophic, as the blaze quickly consumed the dry, centuries-old oak beams.

Beyond technical issues, the human element of the restoration project was also examined. The workforce included a mix of highly skilled artisans and laborers, but accidents are an inherent risk in such complex operations. Investigators interviewed workers, supervisors, and project managers to determine if negligence or lapses in protocol played a role. While no conclusive evidence of intentional wrongdoing emerged, the inquiry raised concerns about the challenges of coordinating such a large-scale project and ensuring strict adherence to safety standards.

One controversial aspect of the investigation was the use of lead in the cathedral's construction and restoration. The roof and spire contained massive quantities of lead, much of which melted in the fire, releasing toxic particles into the air. Some speculated that improper handling of this material during restoration work could have contributed to the fire's ignition or rapid spread. However, this theory remained speculative, as no direct link between the lead and the fire's origin was found.

As the investigation unfolded, theories beyond accidental causes also surfaced. Could the fire have been the result of arson? Given Notre-Dame's symbolic significance, the idea of deliberate sabotage could not be ignored. However, authorities were quick to state that no evidence of arson had been discovered. Surveillance footage and eyewitness accounts supported the conclusion that the fire was unintentional, though this did little to quell public speculation.

The lack of definitive answers led to frustration and finger-pointing. Critics accused the restoration project's managers of negligence, questioning whether they had adequately prepared for the risks associated with their work. Others argued that the fire was a tragic consequence of underfunding and years of deferred maintenance, which had left the cathedral vulnerable to such an event. Notre-Dame's deteriorating state before the restoration had been well-documented, with missing pieces of stone, crumbling gargoyles, and weakened structures. While the restoration was intended to address these issues, it also introduced new risks, which some felt had not been adequately mitigated.

Amid the search for answers, the fire became a symbol of broader issues in cultural heritage preservation. Notre-Dame was not the first historic monument to suffer from a catastrophic fire, and experts around the world warned that similar tragedies could occur elsewhere if lessons were not learned. The investigation into the fire highlighted the delicate balance between preserving history and protecting it from modern dangers—a challenge that extends far beyond the walls of Notre-Dame.

By the time the official investigation concluded, the fire's cause was officially deemed accidental. While multiple factors likely contributed—ranging from electrical issues to human error—no single cause could be definitively identified. This conclusion, while practical, left many questions unanswered, adding an air of lingering mystery to an already tragic event.

Despite the uncertainties, the investigation brought to light the immense complexity of maintaining and restoring a structure like Notre-Dame. It underscored the need for stricter safety protocols, more robust fire detection systems, and increased funding for heritage preservation. It also served as a reminder of the fragility of even the most enduring monuments, highlighting the importance of vigilance and care in their stewardship.

For Parisians and people around the world, the investigation into the fire's cause was not just about finding answers—it was about understanding how something so devastating could happen to a symbol so beloved. While the exact sequence of events may never be fully known, the tragedy of April 15, 2019, has become a call to action, inspiring renewed efforts to protect the cultural treasures that connect us to our past and to each other.

3. Saving Notre-Dame: The Heroes on the Scene

As the flames devoured Notre-Dame de Paris on the night of April 15, 2019, the world watched in horror. For centuries, the cathedral had stood as a symbol of resilience, faith, and beauty, surviving wars, revolutions, and the passage of time. Yet, in just a few hours, it seemed on the verge of collapse. In the face of this catastrophe, a group of extraordinary individuals stepped forward, risking everything to save one of humanity's most treasured landmarks. Their bravery and determination turned the tide on a night that could have ended in complete devastation.

The first alarm sounded at 6:18 PM, but the initial inspection found no signs of fire. It wasn't until a second alarm rang 23 minutes later that the extent of the crisis became clear. By then, flames had taken hold in the attic, fueled by the centuries-old wooden beams known as "the forest." The fire spread rapidly, feeding on the dry timber and climbing toward the spire, which soon became a towering inferno visible across Paris.

Firefighters arrived on the scene quickly, but they were immediately confronted with an immense challenge. Notre-Dame's medieval design, with its intricate stonework, narrow staircases, and high ceilings, made it nearly impossible to navigate. The sheer scale of the fire was daunting, and the structural integrity of the building was at risk. If the flames reached the twin bell towers, the wooden framework supporting the bells could ignite, potentially causing the entire facade to collapse. Saving the cathedral required a delicate balance: extinguish the fire without causing further damage to the fragile structure.

Led by General Jean-Claude Gallet of the Paris Fire Brigade, over 400 firefighters launched a coordinated effort to combat the blaze. As flames engulfed the roof and the spire collapsed in a fiery cascade, the firefighters focused on protecting the cathedral's most vulnerable and vital areas. The stakes were immeasurable—not just for Paris, but for the world.

Inside the cathedral, conditions were treacherous. The heat was overwhelming, and thick smoke filled the air, making it nearly impossible to see or breathe. Yet, teams of firefighters pressed forward, using thermal imaging cameras to locate the hottest areas and guide their efforts. Their mission was clear: prevent the fire from reaching the bell towers at all costs.

To achieve this, firefighters climbed into the towers themselves, hauling hoses and equipment through narrow, winding staircases. If the fire had reached these areas, the bells' collapse could have brought down the entire structure, taking with it centuries of history and art. Their efforts paid off; by creating a defensive barrier around the towers, they managed to stop the fire from spreading further.

While the fire brigade battled the flames, another group of heroes worked to save Notre-Dame's priceless artifacts and relics. Inside the cathedral, clergy members, museum staff, and volunteers formed human chains to carry out irreplaceable treasures. Among the items rescued were the Crown of Thorns, believed to have been worn by Jesus Christ during the crucifixion, and the Tunic of Saint Louis, a relic associated with King Louis IX. The quick thinking and bravery of these individuals ensured that the spiritual and historical legacy of Notre-Dame was preserved, even as the building itself faced destruction.

One particularly moving moment came when Father Jean-Marc Fournier, the chaplain of the Paris Fire Brigade, entered the cathedral to recover the Blessed Sacrament and the Crown of Thorns. Fournier, known for his courage during the Bataclan terrorist attack in 2015, insisted on returning to the burning structure to retrieve these sacred items. His actions were a powerful reminder of the deep connection between Notre-Dame and the people who cherish it.

Outside, as night fell over Paris, thousands of onlookers gathered along the Seine, their faces illuminated by the orange glow of the fire. Some wept openly, others prayed, and many sang hymns, their voices rising in defiance of the destruction before them. The crowd's unity and determination mirrored the efforts of the firefighters and volunteers inside. Notre-Dame was more than a building; it was a living symbol of their history, their culture, and their faith.

Despite the immense challenges, the firefighters' strategy began to work. By midnight, the flames had been largely contained, though the roof and spire were lost, and much of the attic had been reduced to ash. The great stone walls, however, remained standing, a testament to the ingenuity of the medieval builders and the tireless efforts of the modern-day heroes who fought to save them.

As dawn broke over Paris on April 16, the full extent of the damage became visible. The roof was gone, replaced by a gaping hole open to the sky. Yet, the twin towers stood tall, the rose windows had survived, and the altar cross gleamed defiantly amidst the debris. The cathedral had been scarred, but it was still standing—a symbol of resilience and hope.

The firefighters who saved Notre-Dame were hailed as heroes, their courage celebrated not just in France but around the world. President Emmanuel Macron visited the scene to thank them personally, pledging that Notre-Dame would be rebuilt. The international response was immediate and overwhelming, with donations pouring in to support the restoration. Amid the grief and loss, there was a renewed sense of unity and determination to preserve what Notre-Dame represented.

For those who fought to save the cathedral, the night of the fire was not just a battle against flames—it was a fight to protect history, culture, and identity. Their actions ensured that future generations would continue to marvel at Notre-Dame, to hear its bells ring out over Paris, and to be inspired by its beauty and resilience.

The heroes of Notre-Dame's fire remind us of the extraordinary things ordinary people can achieve in the face of adversity. Their bravery, determination, and unwavering commitment turned what could have been an irreversible tragedy into a story of hope and renewal. As the cathedral undergoes its painstaking restoration, their efforts remain a testament to the human spirit's capacity to protect and preserve what we hold most dear.

4. The Global Response: Donations and Support

When the flames engulfing Notre-Dame de Paris finally subsided in the early hours of April 16, 2019, the world was left in shock. Images of the collapsed spire, the charred roof, and the smoldering ruins of the cathedral spread across the globe, evoking an outpouring of grief and solidarity. Notre-Dame was not just a symbol of Paris or France; it was a cultural treasure, a masterpiece of human achievement that belonged to the world. In the wake of the tragedy, an extraordinary wave of global support emerged, demonstrating the cathedral's universal significance and the collective determination to see it restored.

The response was immediate and overwhelming. Within hours of the fire, French President Emmanuel Macron addressed the nation, vowing to rebuild Notre-Dame. His words resonated deeply, not only in France but around the world. "We will rebuild Notre-Dame," he declared, "because that is what the French people expect, and because it is our destiny." Macron's pledge set the tone for a massive restoration effort, one that would require resources, expertise, and collaboration on an unprecedented scale.

Donations began pouring in almost as soon as the fire was extinguished. Leading the charge were some of France's wealthiest families and corporations. The Pinault family, owners of the luxury brand conglomerate Kering, pledged €100 million. Not to be outdone, the Arnault family, owners of LVMH, the world's largest luxury goods company, committed €200 million. The Bettencourt family, heirs to the L'Oréal fortune, also pledged €200 million. These staggering sums underscored the cathedral's significance not only as a cultural icon but as a source of national pride.

The generosity was not limited to France. Governments, organizations, and individuals from around the world stepped forward to contribute. The Vatican expressed its sorrow and solidarity, and the Pope urged Catholics to support the restoration. In the United States, the French Heritage Society launched a fundraising campaign, while individuals and companies alike made significant contributions. In total, donations from around the globe quickly surpassed €1 billion, a testament to the deep connection people felt to Notre-Dame.

However, the outpouring of generosity also sparked controversy and debate. Some questioned why such immense sums were being directed toward a building when pressing global issues—poverty, climate change, and humanitarian crises—remained underfunded. Critics pointed out the disparity between the rapid mobilization of resources for Notre-Dame and the slow response to disasters affecting vulnerable communities. This tension highlighted the complex relationship between cultural heritage and social priorities, raising important questions about how society allocates its resources and attention.

Despite these debates, the global response to Notre-Dame's fire revealed a shared recognition of the importance of preserving cultural heritage. For many, the cathedral represented more than a physical structure; it was a symbol of human creativity, resilience, and the enduring power of faith and art. The fire had destroyed much of Notre-Dame's roof and spire, but its walls, towers, and rose windows remained intact, a reminder of its strength and significance. The restoration effort became a rallying point, a chance for people around the world to contribute to something greater than themselves.

The logistical challenges of restoring Notre-Dame were immense. The fire had caused extensive damage not only to the structure but also to the delicate interior, which was coated in soot and debris. The roof, once supported by a complex network of wooden beams, was gone, leaving the cathedral vulnerable to the elements. The spire, a 19th-century addition by architect Eugène Viollet-le-Duc, had collapsed entirely, taking with it some of the cathedral's iconic statues and carvings. Rebuilding these elements required expertise, funding, and time.

Fortunately, the outpouring of support included not only financial contributions but also offers of technical assistance. Architects, engineers, and craftsmen from around the world volunteered their skills to the restoration effort. Countries with rich traditions of Gothic architecture, such as Germany and the United Kingdom, offered expertise in stonework and stained-glass restoration. Modern technology, including 3D scanning and digital modeling, played a crucial role in planning the reconstruction. These tools allowed restorers to recreate lost elements with incredible accuracy, ensuring that the rebuilt Notre-Dame would remain faithful to its original design.

The international response also included symbolic gestures that underscored the cathedral's global significance. In Poland, church bells rang in solidarity with Notre-Dame. In the United States, cities such as New York and San Francisco illuminated their landmarks in the colors of the French flag. These acts of unity highlighted the deep connections between people and places, a reminder that Notre-Dame's loss was felt far beyond the borders of France.

Amid the tragedy, the global response to Notre-Dame's fire offered a powerful narrative of hope and resilience. It demonstrated humanity's capacity to come together in the face of loss, to protect and preserve what is most precious. The fire was a devastating blow, but it also served as a reminder of the values that Notre-Dame represents: creativity, perseverance, and the enduring power of beauty to inspire and uplift.

As the restoration effort progresses, the story of Notre-Dame continues to evolve. The global response to the fire remains a defining chapter in this story, a testament to the cathedral's ability to unite people across cultures and generations. For those who contributed to the restoration—whether through donations, expertise, or simply their words of support—Notre-Dame's survival is a shared achievement, a symbol of what can be accomplished when the world comes together.

In the end, the fire of April 15, 2019, was not the end of Notre-Dame's story. It was a new beginning, a chance to reaffirm its place in the hearts of millions and to ensure that it will continue to inspire for centuries to come. The global response to the fire stands as a testament to the enduring power of Notre-Dame, a reminder that some symbols are too important to lose and that, even in the face of tragedy, hope and determination can prevail.

Chapter 5: What the Fire Revealed : Discoveries Beneath the Ashes

1.Ancient Relics and Artifacts Unearthed

The fire that consumed much of Notre-Dame de Paris on April 15, 2019, was a tragedy of immense proportions, but amid the ashes, it also became an opportunity for discovery. As the restoration process began, archaeologists, historians, and conservationists were granted an unprecedented chance to explore parts of the cathedral that had remained hidden for centuries. Beneath the charred remains of the roof and spire, the fire revealed relics and artifacts that deepened our understanding of Notre-Dame's history, its construction, and its enduring significance.

Among the most notable discoveries were fragments of the cathedral's original construction materials. As workers cleared debris from the site, they unearthed sections of ancient stonework, iron fittings, and wooden beams that had been hidden since the Middle Ages. These materials offered rare insights into the techniques used by the builders of Notre-Dame in the 12th and 13th centuries. For instance, charred remnants of oak beams from the attic—nicknamed "the forest" for the vast number of trees used in its construction—provided valuable information about medieval forestry and carpentry practices. Dendrochronology, the study of tree rings, allowed researchers to date the beams with remarkable precision, shedding light on the specific periods and regions from which the timber was sourced.

In addition to construction materials, several relics and artifacts of religious and cultural significance were recovered. Among the most extraordinary finds were lead caskets discovered buried beneath the cathedral's floor. These caskets, believed to date back to the 14th century, contained human remains, likely those of prominent figures associated with the cathedral. The discovery of these caskets underscored the importance of Notre-Dame not only as a place of worship but also as a site of commemoration and burial for Paris's elite.

One of the most poignant discoveries was the recovery of fragments of the cathedral's original stained glass. While the great rose windows miraculously survived the fire, smaller sections of glass from less prominent windows were damaged or destroyed. During the cleanup, artisans found shards of these centuries-old pieces embedded in the debris. These fragments, with their vivid colors and intricate designs, offered a glimpse into the artistry of medieval glassmakers. Efforts to preserve and study these fragments have provided valuable insights into the techniques used to create Notre-Dame's windows, from the pigments employed to the methods of assembly.

The fire also exposed parts of the cathedral's foundations that had long been obscured. As restoration crews stabilized the structure, they uncovered remnants of the original Romanesque church that had stood on the site before Notre-Dame was built. These foundations, thought to date back to the 4th or 5th century, revealed the long history of sacred worship on the Île de la Cité. The discovery of these earlier structures added a new layer to Notre-Dame's story, connecting it to the ancient roots of Paris itself.

One of the most intriguing finds came from within the spire, which collapsed dramatically during the fire. The spire, a 19th-century addition by architect Eugène Viollet-le-Duc, had contained a lead-covered cavity designed to house relics. During the cleanup, workers recovered the copper rooster that had adorned the top of the spire. Remarkably, inside the rooster were several relics that had been placed there as part of a protective tradition. Among these were a fragment of the Crown of Thorns and relics associated with Saint Denis and Saint Genevieve, the patron saints of Paris. The survival of these items, despite the destruction around them, was seen by many as a symbol of hope and resilience.

In addition to these tangible artifacts, the fire also revealed much about the hidden layers of the cathedral's history. For centuries, parts of Notre-Dame had been altered, repaired, or obscured by later additions, leaving some of its original features hidden from view. The fire, destructive as it was, stripped away some of these layers, exposing elements of the cathedral that had not been seen since its earliest days. For instance, sections of the medieval roof structure, long covered by later modifications, were revealed in the aftermath of the blaze, offering a rare opportunity to study the original design.

The discoveries unearthed after the fire have been both illuminating and bittersweet. Each artifact and relic recovered from the ashes is a reminder of what was lost, but also of the extraordinary craftsmanship and devotion that went into creating Notre-Dame. These finds have sparked renewed interest in the cathedral's history, inspiring efforts to document and preserve its legacy for future generations.

For archaeologists and historians, the process of uncovering these treasures has been a once-in-a-lifetime opportunity. It has allowed them to piece together Notre-Dame's story in ways that would not have been possible otherwise. The discoveries have provided a more complete understanding of the materials, techniques, and traditions that shaped the cathedral, enriching our appreciation of its artistry and significance.

For the public, the revelations beneath the ashes have deepened the emotional connection to Notre-Dame. The artifacts recovered from the fire are not just remnants of the past; they are symbols of the cathedral's enduring spirit. They remind us that Notre-Dame is more than a building—it is a living monument, one that continues to reveal its secrets and inspire awe even in the face of tragedy.

As the restoration of Notre-Dame progresses, the discoveries made in the aftermath of the fire serve as a foundation for its renewal. The lessons learned from these relics and artifacts will guide the efforts to rebuild the cathedral, ensuring that its reconstruction honors the vision of its original creators while preserving its history for future generations. In this way, the fire, though devastating, has also been a catalyst for discovery, a reminder that even in loss, there is the potential for renewal and understanding.

2.Structural Insights: What We Learned About Gothic Engineering

The fire that tore through Notre-Dame de Paris on April 15, 2019, was a devastating event, but it also provided a unique and unprecedented opportunity to study the cathedral's structure in ways that had never before been possible. As architects, engineers, and conservationists began the painstaking process of assessing the damage, they uncovered new insights into the ingenuity of Gothic engineering. These revelations have deepened our understanding of the techniques and principles that allowed medieval builders to create structures that continue to inspire awe centuries later.

One of the most striking discoveries was the resilience of Notre-Dame's stone framework. Despite the intense heat generated by the fire, which reached temperatures of up to 800 degrees Celsius (1,472 degrees Fahrenheit), the primary structure of the cathedral remained largely intact. The limestone walls and vaulted ceilings, which form the skeleton of the building, withstood the flames far better than expected. This durability highlighted the brilliance of Gothic construction methods, which relied on a delicate balance of forces to achieve both stability and aesthetic grace.

The ribbed vaults of the cathedral, a hallmark of Gothic design, played a key role in this resilience. These intricate, web-like structures distribute weight evenly across the walls and columns, reducing the pressure on any single point. During the fire, sections of the roof collapsed, but the ribbed vaults prevented the flames from spreading into the interior of the nave. This containment minimized the damage to the cathedral's interior and protected its invaluable treasures. Engineers studying the aftermath marveled at the effectiveness of this centuries-old design, which demonstrated a level of sophistication that rivaled modern techniques.

Another critical feature of Notre-Dame's engineering was its use of flying buttresses. These external supports, which extend outward from the walls, counteract the lateral thrust of the roof and vaults, allowing the cathedral to achieve its soaring heights without compromising stability. The fire provided a rare opportunity to examine these buttresses in detail, revealing not only their structural role but also the care and precision with which they were crafted. Despite being exposed to intense heat and falling debris, the flying buttresses remained largely unscathed, a testament to their robust design.

The collapse of the spire, however, exposed vulnerabilities in certain aspects of the cathedral's structure. The spire, a 19th-century addition by architect Eugène Viollet-le-Duc, was constructed from a combination of oak and lead. While visually striking, its weight placed additional strain on the cathedral's central framework. When the spire fell, it pierced through the roof and caused localized damage to the stone vaults below. This event highlighted the challenges of integrating later additions with the original Gothic design, underscoring the need for careful consideration in future restoration efforts.

One of the most significant revelations came from the charred remains of the wooden attic, known as "the forest." This vast network of oak beams, many of which dated back to the 12th century, was a marvel of medieval carpentry. Each beam was hewn from a single tree, and the entire structure required a forest's worth of timber to complete. The attic's destruction allowed researchers to study its design in detail, revealing the extraordinary craftsmanship and ingenuity of the builders. The beams were meticulously arranged to maximize strength while minimizing the amount of wood required, a technique that showcased an advanced understanding of load distribution.

The fire also brought attention to the vulnerabilities inherent in Gothic construction. While the stone framework proved remarkably durable, the extensive use of wood in the roof and attic made the structure highly susceptible to fire. This reliance on combustible materials was a necessary compromise for medieval builders, who lacked access to modern materials like steel and concrete. The fire underscored the importance of integrating fire-resistant materials into restoration projects, a challenge that will undoubtedly shape the future of Notre-Dame and other historic structures.

Modern technology played a crucial role in uncovering these structural insights. Laser scanning and 3D modeling, already in use before the fire, provided detailed records of the cathedral's dimensions and features. These digital tools allowed engineers to compare the post-fire structure with its pre-fire condition, identifying areas of weakness and potential instability. The use of drones to survey the damage further enhanced these efforts, providing high-resolution images of hard-to-reach areas such as the roof and spire.

One of the most intriguing aspects of the investigation was the interplay between traditional craftsmanship and modern science. The fire revealed the depth of knowledge possessed by medieval builders, who relied on empirical observation and trial-and-error to perfect their techniques. At the same time, it demonstrated the value of contemporary engineering methods in preserving and understanding historic structures. This collaboration between past and present has not only informed the restoration of Notre-Dame but also provided a blueprint for preserving other monuments around the world.

The lessons learned from Notre-Dame extend beyond the technical. The fire highlighted the profound connection between a building's structure and its symbolism. The soaring arches, intricate vaults, and delicate buttresses of Notre-Dame are not merely feats of engineering; they are expressions of faith, creativity, and a desire to transcend the earthly. The fact that these elements endured such a catastrophic event speaks to the enduring power of the human spirit to create and protect what is most cherished.

As the restoration of Notre-Dame continues, the structural insights gained from the fire will play a vital role in shaping its future. Engineers and architects are exploring ways to incorporate modern materials and techniques while remaining faithful to the cathedral's original design. The challenge is not simply to rebuild what was lost but to honor the vision of the medieval builders who created Notre-Dame as a testament to their ingenuity and devotion.

The fire of 2019 was a tragedy, but it also provided an opportunity to deepen our understanding of Gothic engineering and to celebrate the brilliance of those who built Notre-Dame. Their legacy endures not only in the surviving structure but also in the knowledge and inspiration they have passed on to future generations. Notre-Dame is more than a cathedral; it is a living testament to the power of human creativity, a reminder that even in the face of destruction, there is always the potential for discovery and renewal.

3.Secrets of the Roof and Spire

Before the fire of April 15, 2019, the roof and spire of Notre-Dame de Paris were often overlooked, overshadowed by the cathedral's iconic facade and grand interiors. Yet, these elements were marvels of engineering and artistry in their own right, embodying centuries of craftsmanship and creativity. The fire, while devastating, revealed hidden secrets about these structures, offering a deeper understanding of their construction, symbolism, and significance.

The roof of Notre-Dame, affectionately known as "the forest," was one of the most extraordinary features of the cathedral. Constructed in the 12th and 13th centuries, it earned its nickname from the sheer quantity of oak used— each beam hewn from a single tree. In total, it required an entire forest to provide the timber for the lattice of beams that supported the lead-covered roof. This intricate network was an engineering masterpiece, designed to distribute the immense weight of the roof evenly across the stone walls and flying buttresses.

Medieval builders faced the challenge of constructing a roof that was both sturdy and light enough not to compromise the cathedral's verticality. To achieve this, they employed innovative techniques, crafting a wooden framework that was both flexible and strong. The beams were fitted together without the use of nails, relying instead on precision carpentry and mortise-and-tenon joints. This approach allowed the structure to adapt to slight movements caused by changes in temperature and humidity, preserving its integrity for centuries.

The fire, however, exposed the vulnerability of this ancient craftsmanship. The oak beams, dry from centuries of exposure, ignited quickly and burned intensely, creating an inferno that consumed the entire roof in a matter of hours. As the flames roared, they melted the lead sheeting that had covered the roof, sending molten streams cascading into the nave below. This dramatic destruction was a stark reminder of the delicate balance between beauty and fragility that defines Gothic architecture.

Above the roof stood the spire, a 19th-century addition by architect Eugène Viollet-le-Duc. Rising 93 meters (305 feet) above the ground, the spire was both a tribute to the cathedral's medieval origins and a bold statement of 19th-century Gothic Revival aesthetics. Viollet-le-Duc designed the spire to replace an earlier structure that had been removed in the 18th century due to instability. His creation was a marvel of its time, constructed from oak and covered in lead to ensure durability and resistance to the elements.

The spire was more than an architectural feature; it was imbued with profound symbolism. At its peak, it bore a copper rooster containing sacred relics, including a fragment of the Crown of Thorns and relics of Saint Denis and Saint Genevieve, the patron saints of Paris. This rooster was believed to act as a spiritual lightning rod, protecting the cathedral and the city below from harm. The inclusion of these relics reflected the deep intertwining of faith and artistry that defined Notre-Dame.

The spire's collapse during the fire was one of the most heart-wrenching moments of the tragedy. As the flames consumed its wooden core, the structure weakened until it finally toppled, crashing through the roof and into the nave. For many watching, this dramatic fall symbolized the loss of a piece of history. Yet, amid the devastation, the spire's destruction also revealed hidden details about its construction and the materials used by Viollet-le-Duc.

In the aftermath of the fire, workers recovered the copper rooster from the rubble, remarkably intact despite the collapse. Inside, the relics were found to have survived as well, a small but significant victory in the face of such overwhelming loss. The discovery of these relics underscored the care and reverence with which the spire had been constructed, connecting the cathedral's past to its present in a powerful way.

The fire also prompted new studies of the roof and spire, shedding light on aspects of their design that had long been hidden from view. For example, the lead sheeting that covered the roof was found to have been meticulously crafted and layered, providing insights into the techniques and materials available to medieval builders. Similarly, the intricate carvings and decorations on the spire, many of which were previously inaccessible, were documented in detail, preserving their legacy for future generations.

Modern technology played a crucial role in these discoveries. 3D scans and digital models, created before the fire as part of a conservation effort, became invaluable tools for understanding the roof and spire's original construction. These records allowed architects and engineers to study the structures in unprecedented detail, revealing the brilliance of their design and the challenges of their restoration.

The fire also reignited debates about how best to approach the restoration of the roof and spire. Should they be rebuilt exactly as they were, preserving their historical authenticity? Or should modern materials and techniques be used to enhance their safety and durability? These questions sparked passionate discussions among architects, historians, and the public, reflecting the deep connection people feel to Notre-Dame.

For all the devastation it caused, the fire of 2019 illuminated the incredible ingenuity of the medieval and 19th-century builders who crafted the roof and spire of Notre-Dame. Their work, though fragile, was a testament to the power of human creativity and the enduring appeal of Gothic architecture. The secrets revealed in the aftermath of the fire have enriched our understanding of these structures, ensuring that their legacy will continue to inspire awe and admiration for generations to come.

As Notre-Dame undergoes its restoration, the lessons learned from the roof and spire will guide the efforts to rebuild them. The challenge is not only to recreate what was lost but to honor the vision and skill of the builders who came before. In doing so, the roof and spire of Notre-Dame will once again stand as symbols of resilience and renewal, a reminder of the enduring spirit of one of the world's greatest architectural treasures.

4.How the Fire Changed Archaeological Perspectives

Chapter 6: Mysteries of the Cathedral : Unanswered Questions and Theories

1. The Legend of the Holy Grail and Notre-Dame

The catastrophic fire that engulfed Notre-Dame de Paris on April 15, 2019, was a moment of profound loss, yet it also marked a turning point in the way we approach archaeology, heritage preservation, and the understanding of historical structures. As flames consumed the iconic cathedral's roof and spire, exposing its inner framework and hidden features, the fire inadvertently created a unique opportunity for archaeologists and historians to explore Notre-Dame in ways that had never been possible before. The event not only revealed new insights into the cathedral's past but also reshaped the methodologies and philosophies of those dedicated to preserving cultural heritage.

Notre-Dame had long been studied and celebrated as a masterpiece of Gothic architecture, but much of its structure had remained inaccessible, hidden beneath layers of renovation and centuries of additions. The fire stripped away many of these layers, revealing elements of the cathedral's construction and history that had been obscured for generations. For archaeologists, this was both a tragedy and an unprecedented chance to study Notre-Dame as a living historical document.

One of the most significant shifts in perspective was the recognition of the cathedral as a dynamic, evolving structure rather than a static monument. The fire exposed materials and techniques from different periods of Notre-Dame's history, highlighting the ways in which it had been modified and adapted over the centuries. Layers of stonework revealed subtle changes in style and craftsmanship, reflecting the influence of different eras and the evolving needs of the cathedral's caretakers. From the original 12th-century foundation to 19th-century restorations by Eugène Viollet-le-Duc, Notre-Dame's history was written in its very fabric.

The charred remains of the wooden roof, known as "the forest," became a focal point of study. While the destruction of the roof was a devastating loss, it also provided a rare opportunity to examine the medieval carpentry techniques used in its construction. Each beam, hewn from a single oak tree, bore the marks of the craftsmen who shaped it centuries ago. Dendrochronology, the study of tree rings, allowed researchers to date the beams and trace their origins, offering insights into medieval forestry practices and resource management. The intricate lattice of the roof, with its interlocking beams and joints, revealed the ingenuity of the builders who designed it to support immense weight while remaining flexible enough to withstand environmental stresses.

The collapse of the spire, while heartbreaking, also opened new avenues of exploration. Viollet-le-Duc's 19th-century addition, a masterpiece of Gothic Revival architecture, had long been admired from afar but was now accessible for detailed study. The spire's construction methods, materials, and even the copper rooster containing sacred relics were examined in unprecedented detail. These findings not only deepened our understanding of the spire itself but also provided valuable data for its eventual reconstruction.

The fire also uncovered elements of Notre-Dame's earlier history that had been hidden beneath the surface. During stabilization efforts, workers discovered a lead sarcophagus buried beneath the floor of the nave. The coffin, believed to date back to the 14th century, contained human remains and artifacts, shedding light on the individuals who were interred at the cathedral during its long history. Such discoveries underscored Notre-Dame's role not just as a place of worship but as a repository of Parisian history, connecting generations of people to the sacred space.

Another profound impact of the fire was the way it reshaped the approach to preservation and reconstruction. The devastation forced archaeologists and conservationists to grapple with difficult questions about authenticity, restoration, and the integration of modern technology into historic structures. Should Notre-Dame be restored exactly as it was, or should modern materials and techniques be used to ensure its future resilience? The debate illuminated the delicate balance between preserving the past and preparing for the future, challenging traditional notions of heritage conservation.

Modern technology played a critical role in the post-fire analysis, setting new standards for archaeological study. High-resolution 3D scans of Notre-Dame, created before the fire, became invaluable tools for understanding the extent of the damage and planning the restoration. These scans, combined with drone footage and thermal imaging, allowed experts to map the cathedral in extraordinary detail, revealing weaknesses and hidden features that had gone unnoticed for centuries. This integration of technology and archaeology marked a significant evolution in the field, demonstrating how digital tools can complement traditional methods.

The fire also prompted a broader reflection on the vulnerability of cultural heritage sites. Notre-Dame's near-destruction served as a stark reminder of the risks posed by neglect, environmental factors, and human activity. It highlighted the importance of proactive preservation efforts, including the use of advanced fire detection systems and the regular assessment of structural integrity. These lessons resonated beyond Notre-Dame, influencing policies and practices for protecting historic landmarks around the world.

Perhaps the most profound change in archaeological perspectives was the recognition of the emotional and symbolic significance of Notre-Dame. The fire revealed the deep connection people felt to the cathedral, not just as an architectural masterpiece but as a cultural and spiritual touchstone. This collective sense of loss and determination to rebuild underscored the importance of archaeology as a means of preserving not just physical structures but the stories and identities they embody.

For those who study and care for historic sites, the fire of 2019 became a catalyst for innovation and introspection. It demonstrated the resilience of human creativity and the enduring power of cultural heritage to unite people across boundaries of time and space. The discoveries made in the aftermath of the fire have enriched our understanding of Notre-Dame and its history, while also inspiring new approaches to preservation and restoration.

As Notre-Dame rises from the ashes, it carries with it the lessons learned from its near-destruction. The fire has transformed the cathedral from a static monument into a dynamic symbol of renewal, reminding us that history is not fixed but continually evolving. For archaeologists, historians, and the public, the tragedy of the fire has deepened our connection to Notre-Dame and our appreciation for the ingenuity and vision of those who built and cared for it across the centuries.

In the end, the fire of 2019 was not just a loss—it was an opportunity to see Notre-Dame with new eyes, to uncover its secrets, and to ensure that its legacy endures for generations to come. This transformation, born out of tragedy, has reshaped the way we understand and protect the cultural treasures that connect us to our shared past.

2.Underground Tunnels: Fact or Fiction?

Beneath the grand facade of Notre-Dame de Paris lies a network of mysteries as intricate as the cathedral's Gothic architecture. Among the most persistent legends is the existence of underground tunnels—hidden passageways that extend beneath the cathedral and possibly connect it to other parts of Paris. These tales of secret corridors, shrouded in mystery, have captured the imaginations of historians, explorers, and conspiracy theorists for centuries. But how much of this legend is rooted in fact, and how much is the product of myth and speculation?

The story of underground tunnels at Notre-Dame begins with the geography of the Île de la Cité, the ancient heart of Paris. Long before the cathedral was built, the island served as a hub for Roman settlements, leaving behind layers of ruins buried beneath the modern city. Excavations conducted in the 20th century unearthed remnants of Roman streets, baths, and fortifications, now preserved in the archaeological crypt beneath the cathedral square. These findings hint at the historical complexity of the site and suggest the possibility of undiscovered structures beneath the surface.

Notre-Dame itself was constructed atop these ancient foundations, incorporating the existing topography into its design. Medieval builders were known for their ingenuity, often creating subterranean spaces to support massive structures or store essential materials. At Notre-Dame, the need for stability on an island prone to flooding likely necessitated deep foundations and drainage systems. These practical concerns could easily have given rise to legends of tunnels, as later generations interpreted these features as something more mysterious.

One of the most compelling pieces of evidence supporting the existence of underground spaces is the crypt beneath Notre-Dame. This subterranean chamber, accessible to the public today, was rediscovered during 20th-century renovations. It contains not only Roman remains but also medieval artifacts and architectural fragments. While the crypt is primarily an archaeological site, its existence demonstrates the layers of history hidden beneath the cathedral and invites speculation about what else might lie undiscovered.

Beyond the crypt, stories of tunnels connecting Notre-Dame to other parts of Paris have persisted for centuries. One popular theory suggests that a series of passageways link the cathedral to the nearby Conciergerie, once a royal palace and later a notorious prison. During the French Revolution, when Notre-Dame was repurposed as the Temple of Reason, it is said that revolutionaries used these tunnels to transport prisoners or treasures. However, no concrete evidence of such a connection has ever been found, leaving the theory in the realm of folklore.

Another enduring legend involves the Paris Catacombs, the sprawling network of ossuaries beneath the city. While the catacombs are located far from Notre-Dame, some believe that forgotten tunnels could connect the two, creating a secret route through the depths of Paris. This idea has fueled the imaginations of adventurers and urban explorers, but experts remain skeptical. The catacombs, constructed in the 18th century to alleviate overcrowded cemeteries, were never intended to link to the Île de la Cité. Still, the idea of a hidden connection persists, blending fact and fiction into a tantalizing mystery.

The role of Notre-Dame during times of conflict has also contributed to the tunnel legend. During the medieval period, cathedrals often served as sanctuaries and strongholds, their massive walls and elevated positions offering protection in times of siege. In this context, the idea of secret escape routes or storage tunnels beneath Notre-Dame seems plausible. Later, during World War II, Paris became a hub of resistance activity, and Notre-Dame, like other landmarks, was rumored to house secret hideouts or passageways used by the French Resistance. While these stories are difficult to verify, they reflect the symbolic importance of Notre-Dame as a place of refuge and resilience.

Modern technology has provided new tools for exploring these mysteries. Ground-penetrating radar and 3D mapping techniques have been used to study the area around Notre-Dame, revealing the complex layering of structures beneath the cathedral and the Île de la Cité. While no definitive tunnels have been confirmed, these studies have uncovered anomalies and voids in the ground, suggesting the presence of unexplored spaces. Whether these are natural cavities, remnants of ancient construction, or true tunnels remains an open question.

The fire of 2019 added a new chapter to the story of Notre-Dame's underground mysteries. As archaeologists and engineers worked to stabilize the cathedral's structure, they gained access to areas that had been hidden for centuries. This work led to the discovery of a lead sarcophagus and other relics beneath the floor of the nave, sparking renewed interest in the cathedral's subterranean secrets. While no tunnels were uncovered, these findings reinforced the idea that Notre-Dame's foundations hold more stories waiting to be told.

For some, the absence of concrete evidence only adds to the allure of the tunnel legend. The idea of hidden passageways beneath Notre-Dame taps into a universal fascination with the unseen, the forgotten, and the possibility of discovery. It evokes a sense of wonder, drawing people to imagine what might lie beneath one of the world's most famous landmarks. Whether fact or fiction, these stories remind us that Notre-Dame is not just a building but a repository of history, myth, and imagination.

In the end, the question of underground tunnels at Notre-Dame remains unresolved, a tantalizing mystery that invites further exploration. While historians and archaeologists continue to study the site, the legend endures, blending the boundaries between history and myth. Whether these tunnels are ever found or remain a figment of collective imagination, they are a testament to Notre-Dame's power to inspire curiosity and wonder.

As we reflect on the cathedral's history, both above and below ground, one thing is certain: Notre-Dame's secrets are as enduring as its stone walls, and its mysteries will continue to captivate generations to come.

3. The Enigma of the Missing Treasures

For centuries, Notre-Dame de Paris has been a repository of priceless artifacts, sacred relics, and historical treasures. Yet, the cathedral's long history has also been marked by periods of turmoil and upheaval, during which some of its treasures vanished without a trace. These missing artifacts have given rise to countless theories, from theft and mismanagement to deliberate concealment. The mystery of Notre-Dame's missing treasures remains one of its most intriguing stories, blending fact, speculation, and the enduring allure of the unknown.

The story of Notre-Dame's missing treasures begins with its role as a spiritual and cultural hub. Since its completion in the 13th century, the cathedral has been a center for religious devotion, housing relics and artifacts of immense significance to the Christian faith. Among its most famous treasures was the Crown of Thorns, believed to have been worn by Jesus Christ during his crucifixion. Acquired by King Louis IX (later Saint Louis) in the 13th century, the Crown was enshrined in the Sainte-Chapelle before being moved to Notre-Dame. The cathedral also housed relics of saints, precious chalices, ornate vestments, and other ceremonial objects. These items were not merely decorative; they were central to the rituals and traditions of the Church.

However, Notre-Dame's treasures were not immune to the forces of history. The French Revolution, which swept through Paris in the late 18th century, marked one of the darkest periods for the cathedral's collection. Revolutionaries, driven by a desire to overthrow the monarchy and dismantle the power of the Church, targeted Notre-Dame as a symbol of the old regime. Many of the cathedral's treasures were seized, melted down, or sold to fund the revolutionary cause. The Crown of Thorns and other key relics were spared, thanks to the efforts of clergy and loyalists who hid them or transferred them to safer locations. Still, a significant portion of the cathedral's wealth disappeared during this period, its fate unknown.

Some of these missing treasures have resurfaced over the years, discovered in private collections, auction houses, or other unexpected places. For example, in the 19th century, several ornate reliquaries believed to have originated from Notre-Dame were identified in museums and private collections across Europe. These discoveries have raised questions about how such items ended up outside the cathedral and whether others remain hidden, waiting to be uncovered.

Theories about the missing treasures abound. One of the most popular suggests that some items were deliberately concealed by clergy or loyalists during periods of unrest, hidden within the cathedral itself or buried in secret locations nearby. Notre-Dame's vast size, with its crypt, chapels, and labyrinthine passages, provides countless hiding places that could have served as temporary vaults for precious items. While modern restoration efforts have uncovered many fascinating artifacts, no definitive trove of hidden treasures has been found, leaving the theory tantalizingly unresolved.

Another theory posits that some treasures were smuggled out of France during the Revolution or later conflicts, sold to collectors or museums in other countries. The international art market of the 19th and early 20th centuries was notorious for its lack of regulation, making it possible for valuable artifacts to change hands without documentation. The possibility that Notre-Dame's lost treasures could be scattered around the globe adds a layer of intrigue to their story, turning them into a kind of cultural detective case.

The 2019 fire that devastated Notre-Dame reignited interest in the mystery of its missing treasures. As archaeologists and restoration teams combed through the debris, they discovered relics, architectural fragments, and even human remains, deepening our understanding of the cathedral's history. These findings raised hopes that some of the missing treasures might yet be recovered, hidden within the cathedral's walls or buried beneath its foundations. While no major discoveries were made, the fire reminded the world of Notre-Dame's capacity to surprise and its enduring connection to the past.

Modern technology has added a new dimension to the search for the missing treasures. Tools such as ground-penetrating radar and 3D mapping have allowed researchers to study the cathedral's structure in unprecedented detail, identifying voids and anomalies that might indicate hidden spaces. These methods, combined with archival research and historical records, have the potential to shed new light on the fate of Notre-Dame's lost artifacts.

The mystery of the missing treasures also speaks to the broader challenges of heritage preservation. Over its long history, Notre-Dame has been subject to wars, revolutions, and environmental damage, each event leaving its mark on the cathedral and its collection. The loss of treasures is not unique to Notre-Dame; it is a reminder of the fragility of cultural heritage and the importance of safeguarding it for future generations.

For the people of Paris and the millions who visit Notre-Dame each year, the missing treasures are more than a historical curiosity. They represent a link to the cathedral's storied past, a reminder of its role as a witness to centuries of human achievement and struggle. The search for these treasures is not just about recovering objects; it is about preserving the stories and traditions they embody, ensuring that Notre-Dame continues to inspire and connect people across time and space.

In the end, the enigma of Notre-Dame's missing treasures may never be fully solved. Some items may be lost forever, their stories consigned to history. Others may resurface in the most unexpected ways, offering new insights and deepening our connection to the cathedral. Regardless of the outcome, the mystery itself is part of Notre-Dame's enduring allure—a reminder that even in a world of advanced technology and exhaustive research, some secrets remain tantalizingly out of reach.

As restoration efforts continue and new discoveries are made, the story of Notre-Dame's missing treasures serves as a testament to the cathedral's resilience and the enduring power of its legacy. Whether hidden in its walls, scattered across the globe, or lost to time, these treasures remain a symbol of the human spirit's capacity for creation, preservation, and wonder.

4.Myths and Urban Legends Surrounding the Fire

The fire that engulfed Notre-Dame de Paris on April 15, 2019, was not only a devastating loss but also a moment that captivated the world. Within hours of the first images of flames leaping from the cathedral's iconic spire, speculation and theories began to swirl. The event gave rise to a flurry of myths and urban legends, fueled by the global reach of social media, the cultural significance of Notre-Dame, and the human tendency to search for meaning in tragedy. These stories, ranging from the plausible to the fantastical, continue to shape public perception of the fire and its aftermath.

One of the most pervasive myths centers on the origins of the fire. While official investigations concluded that the blaze was accidental, likely caused by an electrical fault or a mishap related to ongoing restoration work, conspiracy theories quickly emerged. Some claimed that the fire was an act of arson, possibly linked to anti-Christian sentiment or political unrest. These theories gained traction in certain corners of the internet, despite the lack of evidence. The fire's timing—occurring during Holy Week and amid heightened political tensions in France—added fuel to these speculations. Authorities repeatedly debunked these claims, but the idea of deliberate sabotage continues to linger in the public imagination.

Another popular urban legend suggests that hidden treasures or secrets were uncovered during the fire. Notre-Dame's long history and its status as a repository of religious relics made it a prime candidate for such speculation. Some claimed that the flames exposed forgotten chambers or revealed long-lost artifacts hidden within the cathedral's walls. While archaeologists did make some fascinating discoveries during the restoration process—such as lead sarcophagi and remnants of earlier structures—none matched the dramatic revelations imagined in these stories. Yet, the idea that the fire might have unearthed something extraordinary persists, fueled by Notre-Dame's enduring aura of mystery.

The symbolism of the fire itself also gave rise to myths. For many, the sight of Notre-Dame in flames was more than a physical event—it was a moment loaded with meaning. Some interpreted the fire as a sign of divine displeasure, pointing to the cathedral's declining role in modern religious life. Others saw it as a metaphor for the fragility of cultural heritage in the face of neglect and environmental threats. These interpretations, while not grounded in fact, reflect the deep emotional and symbolic resonance of Notre-Dame and its role as a cultural touchstone.

One of the more fantastical legends to emerge involved the cathedral's gargoyles and chimeras. These grotesque stone figures, long associated with the protection of Notre-Dame, became the subject of imaginative tales in the wake of the fire. Some claimed that the gargoyles had come to life during the blaze, defending the cathedral from further destruction. Others suggested that the figures had been mysteriously unharmed, standing as silent witnesses to the devastation. While these stories are pure fiction, they highlight the way in which Notre-Dame's architecture has inspired a sense of wonder and myth-making for centuries.

Social media played a significant role in spreading and amplifying these myths. As videos and images of the fire went viral, they were accompanied by a flood of commentary, much of it speculative. One particularly striking image—a golden cross gleaming amid the smoky ruins of the cathedral's interior—was shared widely as a symbol of hope and resilience. While the cross's survival was not miraculous (it was made of non-combustible materials), the image took on a life of its own, inspiring countless interpretations and becoming a rallying point for those mourning the fire.

Another myth tied to the fire involves the fate of the Crown of Thorns, one of Notre-Dame's most sacred relics. Early reports suggested that the Crown might have been lost in the blaze, sparking panic among the faithful. When news emerged that the relic had been saved by firefighters and clergy members forming a human chain, the story quickly became one of heroism and divine intervention. While the rescue was indeed remarkable, some accounts exaggerated the peril faced by the relic, adding to its mythic status.

The fire also reignited older legends about Notre-Dame, blending historical myths with contemporary events. Stories of secret Templar treasures, hidden passageways, and esoteric symbols in the cathedral's design resurfaced, now framed in the context of the fire. These tales, while entertaining, often blurred the line between fact and fiction, contributing to the cathedral's mystique but complicating efforts to understand its true history.

Amid the myths and urban legends, one undeniable truth emerged: the fire at Notre-Dame revealed the profound cultural and emotional significance of the cathedral. For millions around the world, the event was more than a physical loss—it was a symbol of human vulnerability, resilience, and the shared desire to preserve beauty and history. The stories that sprang from the fire, whether grounded in fact or born of imagination, reflect the deep connection people feel to Notre-Dame and the role it plays in the collective consciousness.

In the years since the fire, these myths and legends have become part of the broader narrative of Notre-Dame. They serve as a reminder of the cathedral's power to inspire awe and wonder, even in the face of tragedy. While the fire's true causes and consequences are well-documented, the stories that surround it add a layer of richness to its history, ensuring that Notre-Dame remains not just a building but a living symbol of human creativity and endurance.

Ultimately, the myths and urban legends surrounding the fire of Notre-Dame reveal as much about us as they do about the cathedral itself. They speak to our need for meaning, our fascination with the mysterious, and our enduring reverence for places that connect us to the past. Whether these stories are true or imagined, they remind us that Notre-Dame is more than stone and glass—it is a vessel for our dreams, fears, and aspirations, a place where history and myth intertwine.

Chapter 7: Notre-Dame Reimagined : The Future of a Global Icon

1. The Restoration Project: Goals and Challenges

The fire that ravaged Notre-Dame de Paris on April 15, 2019, left the world stunned. The iconic spire had fallen, the roof was destroyed, and the cathedral's interior was shrouded in smoke and ash. Yet, even as the flames were being extinguished, a commitment to rebuild was taking shape. French President Emmanuel Macron declared that Notre-Dame would rise again, setting an ambitious timeline of five years for its restoration. What followed was one of the most complex and scrutinized restoration projects in modern history, a challenge not only of engineering but also of philosophy, artistry, and cultural identity.

The primary goal of the restoration project is to return Notre-Dame to its pre-fire state, preserving its role as a symbol of faith, art, and resilience. To achieve this, the project must balance two seemingly contradictory objectives: remaining faithful to the cathedral's historical integrity while incorporating modern techniques and materials to ensure its future durability. This balancing act has sparked debates among architects, historians, and the public, all of whom have a stake in the fate of one of the world's most beloved landmarks.

From the outset, the restoration team faced immense challenges. The first was stabilizing the structure, which had been weakened by the fire. The intense heat had caused sections of the stone vaulting to crack, while the roof's collapse left the remaining framework vulnerable to the elements. Temporary scaffolding was erected to prevent further damage, and a massive protective canopy was installed to shield the interior from rain and wind. These measures were crucial for preserving what remained of the cathedral, but they also underscored the fragility of the task ahead.

Another immediate priority was assessing the damage and cataloging what could be saved. Archaeologists and engineers worked alongside conservators to sift through the debris, recovering artifacts, fragments of stained glass, and even charred pieces of the original wooden roof. Each discovery provided valuable information about the cathedral's construction and history, guiding decisions about how to proceed with the restoration. Modern technology, including 3D scanning and digital modeling, played a crucial role in this process, allowing the team to document every detail of the cathedral's pre-fire condition.

One of the most contentious aspects of the restoration project has been the question of how to rebuild the spire. Designed by 19th-century architect

Eugène Viollet-le-Duc, the spire was a relatively modern addition to the medieval structure, yet it had become an integral part of Notre-Dame's silhouette. After the fire, some proposed replacing the spire with a contemporary design, arguing that the restoration should reflect the cathedral's ongoing evolution. Others insisted on an exact replica, emphasizing the need to preserve Notre-Dame's historical continuity. Ultimately, the French government decided to rebuild the spire as it was, a decision that honors both Viollet-le-Duc's vision and the public's emotional connection to the original design.

Recreating the roof and spire presents a host of technical challenges. The original roof, known as "the forest," was constructed from a dense lattice of oak beams, many of which dated back to the 12th and 13th centuries. To replicate this structure, the restoration team has sourced oak from sustainable forests across France, ensuring that the new beams match the dimensions and quality of the originals. The lead sheeting that once covered the roof will also be replaced, despite concerns about the material's environmental impact. These decisions reflect a commitment to authenticity, even as they raise practical and ethical questions about the use of traditional materials in a modern context.

The stained-glass windows of Notre-Dame, including the iconic rose windows, are another focal point of the restoration. Miraculously, these masterpieces survived the fire, though they were coated in soot and exposed to extreme heat. Conservators have undertaken the painstaking task of cleaning and restoring each pane, using both traditional methods and cutting-edge technology. The goal is not only to preserve the visual splendor of the windows but also to honor the craftsmanship of the medieval artisans who created them.

Beyond the physical challenges, the restoration project has also sparked broader discussions about Notre-Dame's role in contemporary society. As a religious site, the cathedral holds deep significance for Catholics around the world. As a cultural icon, it represents the artistry and ingenuity of the Gothic era. And as a symbol of resilience, it has come to embody the human spirit's ability to overcome adversity. The restoration must navigate these overlapping identities, ensuring that Notre-Dame continues to inspire and unite people from all walks of life.

One of the most inspiring aspects of the restoration project has been the outpouring of global support. Donations from individuals, corporations, and governments have poured in, reflecting the universal admiration for Notre-Dame. This financial backing has provided the resources necessary to tackle the project's immense scope, but it has also brought with it a sense of responsibility to honor the generosity of those who have contributed.

As the restoration progresses, the team has embraced a collaborative approach, drawing on expertise from around the world. Architects, engineers, conservators, and craftspeople have come together to share their knowledge and skills, creating a project that is as much about human collaboration as it is about architectural preservation. This spirit of unity has become a defining feature of the effort, reinforcing Notre-Dame's status as a global icon.

Despite the progress made, challenges remain. The timeline set by President Macron—reopening the cathedral by 2024—has placed immense pressure on the restoration team. The COVID-19 pandemic added further delays, halting work for months and complicating international collaboration. Yet, the determination to meet this goal remains strong, driven by the desire to restore Notre-Dame not only for its historical and cultural value but also as a symbol of hope for a world that has faced its own trials in recent years.

As the scaffolding begins to come down and Notre-Dame reclaims its place on the Parisian skyline, the restoration project stands as a testament to human ingenuity, perseverance, and the enduring power of cultural heritage. It is a reminder that even in the face of destruction, we have the ability to rebuild, to honor the past while embracing the future.

In many ways, the restoration of Notre-Dame is about more than the cathedral itself. It is about preserving a shared history, fostering a sense of connection, and demonstrating what can be achieved when people come together for a common purpose. When Notre-Dame reopens its doors, it will not only be a celebration of its rebirth but also a reflection of the resilience and creativity that define us as a global community.

2.Integrating Modern Technology with Historical Accuracy

The restoration of Notre-Dame de Paris is not just a journey back in time; it is also a leap into the future. The fire of 2019 destroyed much of the cathedral's roof and spire, leaving behind a mix of ash, debris, and hard questions about how best to rebuild. Should the restoration adhere strictly to the past, or should it embrace the possibilities offered by modern technology? For the architects, engineers, and craftspeople involved, this project has become a delicate balancing act: honoring the historical accuracy of a medieval masterpiece while leveraging cutting-edge tools to ensure its resilience for centuries to come.

Modern technology has played a pivotal role in nearly every aspect of Notre-Dame's restoration, starting with the initial assessment of the damage. In the days following the fire, drones equipped with high-resolution cameras were deployed to capture detailed images of the cathedral's exterior and interior. These images allowed engineers to evaluate the stability of the remaining structure and identify areas of immediate concern, such as cracks in the stone vaults or weakened buttresses. Without this technology, accessing certain parts of the cathedral would have been impossible, given the extent of the destruction and the dangers posed by unstable debris.

One of the most groundbreaking tools used in the restoration process has been 3D laser scanning. Prior to the fire, Notre-Dame had been meticulously documented by art historian Andrew Tallon, who created an extensive 3D model of the cathedral using laser scans. This digital blueprint, accurate to within millimeters, has become an invaluable resource for the restoration team. It provides a precise record of the cathedral's dimensions, materials, and structural details, allowing architects to reconstruct damaged sections with unparalleled accuracy. The scans have also revealed hidden features, such as variations in the thickness of the walls or the subtle asymmetry of the arches, offering new insights into the techniques of medieval builders.

As the restoration progresses, digital modeling continues to guide the process. Engineers and architects have created virtual simulations of the entire structure, enabling them to test the effects of different materials and designs on the cathedral's stability. For example, they have used these models to analyze how the weight of a new roof and spire might affect the stone walls and flying buttresses, ensuring that the restored elements will be both historically accurate and structurally sound. This combination of historical fidelity and modern precision reflects the project's dual commitment to preserving Notre-Dame's legacy while preparing it for the future.

One of the most controversial aspects of integrating modern technology has been the choice of materials for the restoration. The original roof, known as "the forest," was made from oak beams, each one hewn from a single tree. To replicate this structure, the restoration team has sourced oak from sustainable forests across France, but the use of such large quantities of wood has raised environmental concerns. Some have argued that modern materials, such as steel or carbon fiber, could provide a more durable and fire-resistant alternative. However, purists insist that the use of traditional materials is essential to maintaining the authenticity of Notre-Dame's architecture. In the end, the decision to use oak reflects a compromise: a nod to historical accuracy, paired with modern forestry practices that minimize environmental impact.

Modern techniques are also being used to restore Notre-Dame's iconic stained-glass windows, many of which were coated in soot and exposed to extreme heat during the fire. Conservators have employed advanced cleaning methods, including laser technology, to remove layers of dirt and grime without damaging the delicate glass. In some cases, digital imaging has been used to recreate missing sections of the windows, ensuring that the restored designs match the originals as closely as possible. This meticulous work not only preserves the visual splendor of the windows but also honors the craftsmanship of the medieval artisans who created them.

Perhaps the most visible application of modern technology will be in the reconstruction of the spire. Designed by 19th-century architect Eugène Viollet-le-Duc, the spire was a masterpiece of Gothic Revival architecture, rising 93 meters (305 feet) above the ground. Its collapse during the fire was one of the most heartbreaking moments of the tragedy. Rebuilding the spire presents unique challenges, as it must integrate seamlessly with the medieval structure while meeting contemporary safety standards. Engineers are using 3D modeling and structural analysis to ensure that the new spire will be both historically accurate and capable of withstanding modern environmental pressures, such as wind and temperature fluctuations.

In addition to restoring Notre-Dame's physical structure, modern technology is also enhancing its accessibility and educational value. Digital reconstructions of the cathedral have been made available to the public, allowing people around the world to explore its history and architecture in virtual reality. These digital tools have proven especially valuable during the restoration process, offering a way to engage the public and maintain Notre-Dame's cultural presence even while its doors remain closed.

The integration of modern technology with historical accuracy has also sparked broader philosophical debates about the nature of restoration. Should the goal be to recreate the cathedral exactly as it was, or to adapt it to the needs and values of the present day? This question has been at the heart of discussions about incorporating new features, such as fire-resistant materials or advanced climate control systems, into the restoration. While these additions might deviate from the original design, they also ensure that Notre-Dame can be preserved for future generations, balancing the cathedral's historical significance with its practical needs.

Despite these challenges, the use of modern technology has brought unexpected benefits to the restoration process. It has deepened our understanding of Notre-Dame's construction, revealing the ingenuity of its original builders and the complexity of its design. It has also highlighted the potential of technology to bridge the gap between past and present, offering new ways to connect with and preserve cultural heritage.

As the restoration of Notre-Dame moves forward, it serves as a powerful example of how tradition and innovation can coexist. The project is not just about rebuilding a cathedral; it is about honoring the spirit of creativity and craftsmanship that has defined Notre-Dame for centuries. By integrating modern technology with historical accuracy, the restoration team is ensuring that this global icon will continue to inspire awe and wonder for generations to come.

In the end, the restoration of Notre-Dame is a testament to the enduring power of human ingenuity. It is a reminder that even in the face of destruction, we have the tools and the determination to rebuild, to preserve, and to reimagine. As Notre-Dame rises from the ashes, it stands as a symbol of resilience, creativity, and the timeless bond between history and the future.

3.Debates on the New Design: Tradition vs. Innovation

When Notre-Dame de Paris was engulfed in flames on April 15, 2019, the world mourned the loss of one of its most iconic landmarks. Yet, as the fire was extinguished and the smoke cleared, attention shifted to the future: how would the cathedral be rebuilt? The question ignited a passionate debate that has continued to divide architects, historians, and the public. Should the restoration remain faithful to the original design, preserving every detail as it was before the fire? Or should it embrace innovation, using modern techniques and materials to create something new? This debate between tradition and innovation has become one of the defining narratives of Notre-Dame's restoration.

The fire destroyed much of the cathedral's roof and its spire, which was not part of the original medieval structure but a 19th-century addition by architect Eugène Viollet-le-Duc. Viollet-le-Duc's spire had become an integral part of Notre-Dame's silhouette, rising 93 meters (305 feet) above the Parisian skyline. Its collapse during the fire was a heartbreaking moment, and the question of how to rebuild it quickly became the focal point of the restoration debate.

In the immediate aftermath of the fire, French President Emmanuel Macron announced an ambitious plan: Notre-Dame would be restored and reopened within five years. He also suggested that the restoration could include a contemporary reinterpretation of the spire, sparking widespread speculation and debate. Architects from around the world submitted bold and imaginative proposals, ranging from a glass spire that would reflect the light of the heavens to a vertical garden symbolizing renewal and resilience. These designs captured the imagination of many, offering a vision of Notre-Dame not as a relic of the past but as a living monument that evolves with the times.

Supporters of innovation argued that the fire presented a unique opportunity to reimagine Notre-Dame for the 21st century. They pointed to the history of Gothic architecture itself, which was revolutionary in its time, embracing new techniques and pushing the boundaries of what was possible. To them, restoring the cathedral exactly as it was would be a missed opportunity, a failure to honor the spirit of creativity that had defined Notre-Dame's construction and evolution.

This perspective was shared by some architects and cultural commentators, who saw the fire as a chance to make a statement about resilience and progress. A modern spire, they argued, could symbolize the cathedral's ability to rise from the ashes and reflect contemporary values such as sustainability and innovation. Others suggested that a new design could incorporate modern materials like glass and steel, enhancing the structure's durability while creating a striking visual contrast with its medieval stonework.

However, this vision of innovation faced significant opposition from those who favored a traditional approach. Critics of contemporary designs argued that Notre-Dame's historical and cultural significance lay in its authenticity. To alter its appearance would be to undermine the very qualities that had made it a global icon. For them, the restoration was not an opportunity for reinvention but a solemn duty to preserve the past.

This perspective was shared by many Parisians and historians, who felt a deep emotional connection to Notre-Dame's original design. Viollet-le-Duc's spire, though a later addition, had become a beloved symbol of the cathedral and the city itself. Recreating it exactly as it was would honor its legacy and ensure continuity with the past. Supporters of this approach pointed to other successful restoration projects, such as the rebuilding of Dresden's Frauenkirche after World War II, as examples of how historical accuracy could preserve a monument's integrity.

The debate over tradition versus innovation reached its peak in 2020, when the French government announced its decision: the spire would be rebuilt as an exact replica of Viollet-le-Duc's design. This decision was met with mixed reactions. For those who valued historical accuracy, it was a victory that honored Notre-Dame's heritage. For others, it was a missed opportunity to embrace bold, contemporary ideas.

Even with the decision to recreate the original spire, the debate continues to influence other aspects of the restoration. Questions about materials, techniques, and the inclusion of modern features such as fire-resistant systems and advanced climate control remain at the forefront. While these additions are necessary to ensure the cathedral's long-term survival, they raise questions about how much innovation can be integrated without compromising historical authenticity.

At the heart of this debate is a deeper philosophical question: what does it mean to restore a monument like Notre-Dame? Is the goal to recreate it exactly as it was, preserving a snapshot of history? Or is it to adapt and evolve, allowing the structure to reflect the values and technologies of the present day? Both approaches have merit, and both carry risks. A purely traditional restoration might fail to address the challenges of the future, while an overly innovative one could alienate those who see Notre-Dame as a symbol of timeless beauty.

The debate has also highlighted the role of public opinion in shaping the restoration process. Notre-Dame belongs not only to Paris or France but to the world. Its restoration is being watched by millions, each with their own hopes and expectations. Balancing these perspectives has proven to be one of the most challenging aspects of the project, as stakeholders grapple with the competing demands of history, art, and modernity.

Ultimately, the debate over Notre-Dame's restoration is about more than a single spire or roof. It is a conversation about how we relate to the past and how we envision the future. Notre-Dame is not just a building; it is a living symbol of human creativity, resilience, and faith. Its restoration offers an opportunity to reflect on what we value most in our cultural heritage and how we can preserve it while allowing for renewal and growth.

As the scaffolding rises and the restoration progresses, the debates over tradition and innovation continue to shape the project. Whether the result leans more toward the past or the future, one thing is certain: Notre-Dame will remain a place of inspiration, a monument that embodies the complexity and beauty of human achievement. Its restoration is not just a technical challenge but a profound act of cultural storytelling, one that will resonate for generations to come.

4. The Cathedral's Role in a Changing World

For centuries, Notre-Dame de Paris has been more than just a building. It has been a beacon of faith, an architectural marvel, and a cultural symbol, standing resilient through the passage of time. But as the world changes, so too must the role of this iconic cathedral. The 2019 fire, devastating as it was, forced a global reckoning with Notre-Dame's place in contemporary society. As the world grapples with new challenges—climate change, cultural shifts, and technological advancements—Notre-Dame is poised to redefine itself, ensuring its relevance and resonance in a rapidly evolving world.

In its earliest days, Notre-Dame was built as a house of worship, a physical manifestation of divine grace and human devotion. Its soaring spires, intricate carvings, and luminous stained-glass windows were designed to inspire awe and guide the faithful toward spiritual reflection. Today, the cathedral continues to serve this purpose, but its role as a religious site is now shared with its identity as a global cultural landmark. Millions of visitors each year come not for mass or prayer, but to marvel at its beauty and immerse themselves in its history. This dual identity as a sacred space and a tourist destination presents both opportunities and challenges.

In a world where secularism is on the rise, Notre-Dame's spiritual mission must adapt. While it remains a functioning Catholic cathedral, hosting religious ceremonies and gatherings, it also needs to serve as a space where people of all faiths—or none at all—can find meaning and connection. The restoration of Notre-Dame provides an opportunity to reinforce its role as a place of unity and dialogue, where diverse perspectives can converge in appreciation of its universal significance. This inclusivity is essential for ensuring that Notre-Dame remains relevant to a global audience.

Notre-Dame's role as a cultural ambassador is equally significant. Few landmarks are as universally recognized as this Gothic masterpiece, and its restoration has become a symbol of resilience and collaboration. The global response to the fire—marked by an outpouring of donations and support from individuals, organizations, and governments—underscored the cathedral's ability to transcend national and cultural boundaries. In this way, Notre-Dame has become a reminder of the shared heritage that unites humanity, a testament to the creativity and ingenuity that defines us as a species.

But Notre-Dame's position as a cultural icon also comes with responsibilities. The restoration project has sparked important conversations about the role of heritage sites in addressing contemporary issues, particularly climate change. The fire highlighted the vulnerabilities of historic structures, many of which were not designed to withstand the environmental pressures of the modern world. Rising temperatures, increased humidity, and pollution all pose significant threats to Notre-Dame and similar landmarks. As a result, the restoration effort has placed a strong emphasis on sustainability, exploring ways to incorporate climate-resistant materials and techniques while maintaining historical integrity.

One example of this approach is the sourcing of materials for the roof and spire. The original structure, famously constructed from a dense lattice of oak beams, will be recreated using sustainably harvested timber. This decision reflects a commitment to authenticity, but it also raises questions about balancing tradition with environmental responsibility. Could more modern, durable materials like steel or carbon fiber have been used instead? These debates highlight the complexities of preserving the past in a way that aligns with present-day values.

Technology, too, is reshaping Notre-Dame's role in the world. The restoration project has embraced cutting-edge tools like 3D modeling, virtual reality, and laser scanning to document and reconstruct the cathedral with unparalleled precision. These advancements not only aid in the restoration but also open up new possibilities for engaging with Notre-Dame's history. Virtual tours and digital archives allow people who may never visit Paris to explore the cathedral's art, architecture, and stories from anywhere in the world. In doing so, technology democratizes access to Notre-Dame, ensuring that its cultural and educational value extends far beyond its physical location.

The cathedral's evolving role also reflects broader societal changes. In the face of growing cultural divides and political tensions, Notre-Dame stands as a potential bridge—a place where history, art, and faith converge to inspire dialogue and understanding. Its Gothic arches and rose windows, shaped by centuries of craftsmanship and devotion, remind us of the enduring power of human creativity. As a space that has borne witness to revolutions, wars, and renewals, it offers a sense of continuity in a world that often feels fragmented and uncertain.

Moreover, Notre-Dame has a unique opportunity to contribute to the ongoing conversation about cultural preservation. The fire was a stark reminder of how easily the treasures of the past can be lost, and the restoration effort serves as a case study in resilience and renewal. By sharing the lessons learned from this process, Notre-Dame can inspire similar efforts around the world, helping to safeguard other heritage sites for future generations.

Notre-Dame's role as an educational resource is another area of potential growth. The cathedral has long been a subject of study for historians, architects, and theologians, but the restoration project has expanded its educational impact. Students and researchers now have access to detailed digital models, conservation techniques, and historical insights uncovered during the reconstruction. Public outreach programs, including workshops, lectures, and exhibitions, can further enhance Notre-Dame's role as a center for learning and exploration.

Finally, Notre-Dame's restoration is a powerful symbol of resilience—a reminder that even in the face of tragedy, renewal is possible. The fire that nearly destroyed it could have marked the end of its story, but instead, it has become a new chapter. This narrative of rebirth resonates deeply in a world that continues to face its own challenges, from pandemics to natural disasters. Notre-Dame's survival and restoration inspire hope, demonstrating the strength of collective effort and the enduring value of our shared heritage.

As Notre-Dame moves forward, its role in a changing world will continue to evolve. It will remain a place of worship, a cultural icon, and a beacon of resilience, but it will also take on new responsibilities as a symbol of sustainability, inclusivity, and innovation. The restored cathedral will not just be a monument to the past—it will be a testament to the values and aspirations of the present, a space where history and modernity coexist in harmony.

In many ways, the challenges and opportunities facing Notre-Dame mirror those of the world itself. How do we honor our history while embracing change? How do we preserve the beauty of the past while addressing the needs of the future? Notre-Dame may not have all the answers, but its story offers a powerful example of how we can navigate these questions with grace, creativity, and determination. As it rises once more, Notre-Dame will continue to inspire, reminding us of the enduring power of faith, art, and human connection in an ever-changing world.

Conclusion: The Resilient Heart of Paris

1.Lessons Learned from Notre-Dame's Survival

The fire that consumed much of Notre-Dame de Paris on April 15, 2019, was a moment of profound loss, but it was also a moment of revelation. As the flames receded and the cathedral's charred silhouette came into view, one thing became clear: despite the devastation, much of Notre-Dame had survived. Its twin towers stood tall, its iconic rose windows remained intact, and its vaulted ceilings, though scarred, had largely withstood the inferno. This survival was not a matter of chance but a testament to the ingenuity of its original builders, the resilience of Gothic engineering, and the efforts of those who worked tirelessly to protect it. From this tragedy, we have gained valuable lessons—about architecture, heritage preservation, and our collective responsibility to safeguard the treasures of the past.

One of the most striking lessons from Notre-Dame's survival is the inherent strength of Gothic design. Built in the 12th and 13th centuries, Notre-Dame was a masterpiece of medieval engineering, designed to endure the ravages of time and nature. Its ribbed vaults, flying buttresses, and massive stone walls were not just aesthetic choices but essential elements of its structural integrity. These features allowed the cathedral to distribute weight and withstand pressures that might have caused less sophisticated structures to collapse.

The ribbed vaults, in particular, played a crucial role during the fire. As the wooden roof burned and collapsed, the vaults acted as a protective barrier, preventing the flames from spreading into the nave below. While some sections of the vault were damaged, the majority held firm, preserving the interior and many of its priceless artifacts. This design, a hallmark of Gothic architecture, demonstrated its enduring effectiveness even under the extreme conditions of a modern fire.

Another key lesson lies in the importance of material choice. The stone used in Notre-Dame's construction, primarily limestone from quarries near Paris, proved remarkably resistant to the heat of the fire. While the intense temperatures caused some stones to crack or spall, the overall structure remained stable. This resilience underscores the wisdom of the cathedral's medieval builders, who chose materials not just for their availability but for their durability. It also highlights the need to consider material performance in modern restoration projects, where historical authenticity must be balanced with future resilience.

The fire also underscored the value of modern firefighting techniques and the dedication of those who wield them. The firefighters who responded to the blaze faced immense challenges: soaring flames, intense heat, and the risk of structural collapse. Yet, through their courage and strategy, they managed to save much of the cathedral. By focusing their efforts on the bell towers, they prevented the fire from spreading to the wooden framework that supports the massive bells. Had these towers succumbed, the collapse could have brought down the entire facade, resulting in an even greater loss.

The human element of Notre-Dame's survival extends beyond the firefighters to include the clergy, conservationists, and volunteers who worked to save its treasures. In the chaotic hours of the fire, a human chain was formed to carry out sacred relics, including the Crown of Thorns and the Tunic of Saint Louis. Their swift action not only preserved these irreplaceable items but also reminded the world of the deep emotional and spiritual connection people feel to Notre-Dame. This collective effort serves as a powerful example of what can be achieved when people come together to protect something greater than themselves.

The restoration process that followed the fire has provided its own set of lessons, particularly in the use of technology. Modern tools like 3D scanning, drone imaging, and digital modeling have allowed experts to assess the damage with unprecedented precision. These technologies have not only guided the restoration but have also deepened our understanding of Notre-Dame's construction. For example, the detailed scans revealed subtle asymmetries in the cathedral's design, offering insights into the techniques and challenges faced by its original builders. This marriage of ancient craftsmanship and modern technology demonstrates the potential for innovation to enhance preservation.

Another important lesson from Notre-Dame's survival is the role of cultural heritage in fostering global solidarity. The fire was not just a loss for France; it was a loss for the world. The outpouring of support—from donations to messages of solidarity—highlighted the universal value of Notre-Dame as a symbol of human achievement. This response serves as a reminder that the preservation of cultural landmarks is not just a local responsibility but a global one. Notre-Dame's survival has reinforced the need for international cooperation in protecting heritage sites, many of which face threats from neglect, conflict, and climate change.

The fire also prompted a reexamination of the risks faced by historic structures. While Notre-Dame had a fire detection system in place, it proved insufficient to prevent the disaster. This has led to renewed discussions about how to balance accessibility, security, and preservation in heritage sites. For example, the restoration project has explored the integration of fire-resistant materials and advanced monitoring systems, ensuring that Notre-Dame will be better protected in the future. These measures, though modern, are essential for preserving the cathedral's legacy in a world where environmental and human-made risks are ever-present.

Perhaps the most profound lesson from Notre-Dame's survival is the reminder of the resilience of human creativity and spirit. The cathedral's endurance through the fire, and the collective determination to restore it, speaks to the enduring power of beauty and history to inspire hope. In the face of destruction, Notre-Dame has become a symbol of renewal—a testament to our ability to rebuild and preserve what is most meaningful to us.

As the restoration continues, the lessons learned from Notre-Dame's survival will guide not only the work on the cathedral itself but also efforts to protect other cultural landmarks around the world. These lessons are a call to action, reminding us of the importance of proactive preservation, the value of innovation, and the power of community in safeguarding our shared heritage. They underscore the need to honor the past while preparing for the future, ensuring that monuments like Notre-Dame continue to inspire and connect us for generations to come.

Notre-Dame's survival is more than a story of architectural resilience; it is a story of human resilience. It is a reminder that even in moments of great loss, there is an opportunity for learning, growth, and renewal. As we look to the future, the lessons of Notre-Dame will serve as a guiding light, helping us to navigate the challenges of preserving the treasures of our past in an ever-changing world.

2.The Symbolism of Rebirth and Renewal

The fire that devastated Notre-Dame de Paris in April 2019 was a profound tragedy, but it also ignited a powerful narrative of rebirth and renewal. For centuries, Notre-Dame has been more than just a cathedral—it is a symbol of faith, resilience, and the enduring spirit of humanity. Its ability to rise from the ashes, like a modern-day phoenix, resonates deeply in a world that often feels fraught with loss and uncertainty. The symbolism of Notre-Dame's restoration extends far beyond its walls, offering lessons about renewal, continuity, and the transformative power of hope.

Rebirth is a concept deeply rooted in the history of Notre-Dame itself. The cathedral was constructed in the 12th century during a period of profound transformation in medieval Europe. The Gothic style, characterized by its soaring spires, ribbed vaults, and luminous stained glass, represented a departure from the heavier Romanesque architecture that preceded it. Gothic cathedrals like Notre-Dame were designed to lift the spirit, their vertical lines drawing the eye heavenward and their intricate carvings offering a visual narrative of biblical stories. In many ways, the creation of Notre-Dame was an act of renewal—a bold declaration of faith and human creativity during a time of change.

This theme of renewal continued throughout Notre-Dame's history. The cathedral has undergone numerous transformations, each reflecting the values and challenges of its time. During the French Revolution, it was desecrated and repurposed as the Temple of Reason, its religious artifacts removed or destroyed. Yet, it was restored in the 19th century by Eugène Viollet-le-Duc, whose vision brought new life to its spire, sculptures, and stained glass. These moments of destruction and rebirth are woven into Notre-Dame's story, making its survival through the 2019 fire a continuation of a long tradition of resilience.

The symbolism of Notre-Dame's rebirth is especially powerful in the context of the fire. The sight of flames consuming its roof and toppling its spire was a moment of collective heartbreak. It seemed unthinkable that this architectural masterpiece, which had stood for over 800 years, could be so vulnerable. Yet, in the days that followed, the determination to rebuild emerged as a testament to the enduring power of human spirit and ingenuity. The fire became a catalyst for action, inspiring people from around the world to come together in support of Notre-Dame's restoration.

This collective response speaks to the universal appeal of renewal. For many, Notre-Dame is more than a religious site or a work of art—it is a symbol of shared humanity. Its restoration is not just about rebuilding a structure; it is about reclaiming a piece of our cultural identity, a reminder that even in the face of loss, we have the capacity to create, to rebuild, and to hope. This narrative of renewal resonates on a personal level as well, offering inspiration to those navigating their own challenges and transformations.

The fire and its aftermath have also reframed the way we think about renewal. In many ways, the restoration of Notre-Dame is an opportunity to blend tradition with innovation. The decision to rebuild the spire as an exact replica of Viollet-le-Duc's design reflects a commitment to preserving the past, while the incorporation of modern technology and sustainable materials ensures that the cathedral will endure for future generations. This balance between honoring history and embracing progress is a powerful metaphor for renewal in the modern world—one that acknowledges the importance of the past while looking forward to the future.

Notre-Dame's renewal is not just a physical process; it is also a spiritual one. The cathedral has always been a place of reflection and inspiration, its architecture designed to evoke a sense of wonder and connection to the divine. The fire, while devastating, has deepened this sense of connection. For many, the survival of key elements such as the rose windows and the Crown of Thorns relic is seen as a symbol of hope, a reminder that even in destruction, there is grace. The restoration process has become a spiritual journey in its own right, one that invites people to reflect on themes of loss, resilience, and renewal in their own lives.

The symbolism of Notre-Dame's rebirth extends beyond Paris, offering lessons for the world at large. In an era marked by environmental crises, political divisions, and social upheaval, the story of Notre-Dame is a reminder of the importance of preservation and renewal. It challenges us to think about what we value most—our cultural heritage, our shared humanity, and our ability to overcome adversity—and to consider how we can protect and nurture these things in a changing world.

The global response to Notre-Dame's restoration has highlighted the cathedral's role as a unifying force. The outpouring of donations, expertise, and support from around the world demonstrates the universal appeal of its story. This collective effort to rebuild is itself a symbol of renewal, a testament to what can be achieved when people come together for a common purpose. It reminds us that renewal is not an individual endeavor but a shared journey, one that requires collaboration, compassion, and a vision for the future.

As Notre-Dame rises from the ashes, it carries with it the weight of history and the promise of renewal. Its restoration is a story of resilience, but it is also a story of transformation. The cathedral that emerges will be both familiar and new, a symbol of continuity and change. This duality is at the heart of its power: Notre-Dame is not just a monument to the past but a living symbol of the human capacity for reinvention and growth.

In many ways, the fire of 2019 was a reminder of life's impermanence, but the restoration of Notre-Dame is a testament to the enduring power of renewal. It is a reminder that even in the face of loss, we have the ability to rebuild—not just structures, but connections, communities, and hope. Notre-Dame's story is one of rebirth, and it serves as an inspiration for all who face challenges in their own lives, reminding us that from the ashes of destruction, beauty and strength can emerge.

As the restoration continues, the symbolism of Notre-Dame's rebirth will continue to evolve. It will remain a place of faith and wonder, a reminder of the enduring power of art and architecture to inspire. But it will also stand as a beacon of renewal, a testament to the resilience of humanity and the enduring value of hope. In this way, Notre-Dame's story is not just its own—it is a reflection of our shared journey, a symbol of what it means to rise, to rebuild, and to begin again.

3.Notre-Dame's Legacy in Art and Literature

Notre-Dame de Paris has long been more than a cathedral; it is a muse. Its towering spires, intricate carvings, and solemn presence on the Île de la Cité have inspired artists, writers, and poets for centuries. Few buildings in the world can claim such a profound influence on art and literature, weaving themselves into the fabric of culture and imagination. Notre-Dame is not just a physical monument; it is a symbol, a setting, and a character that continues to resonate in stories and artworks, speaking to universal themes of faith, resilience, and the passage of time.

One of the most iconic works of literature inspired by Notre-Dame is Victor Hugo's *The Hunchback of Notre-Dame* (*Notre-Dame de Paris*), published in 1831. Hugo's novel is inseparable from the cathedral; indeed, one of its primary aims was to draw attention to the neglected state of Gothic architecture in France at the time. Through the story of Quasimodo, the deformed bell-ringer, and Esmeralda, the compassionate gypsy dancer, Hugo brought Notre-Dame to life, portraying it not just as a setting but as a central character. The cathedral looms large over the narrative, its gargoyles, towers, and shadowy nooks serving as a reflection of the characters' inner turmoil and a metaphor for the grandeur and complexity of human existence.

Hugo's portrayal of Notre-Dame had a lasting impact, both on literature and on the cathedral itself. The novel sparked a renewed interest in Gothic architecture, leading to a wave of preservation efforts across Europe. In the case of Notre-Dame, Hugo's work was instrumental in initiating the restoration led by Eugène Viollet-le-Duc, who repaired and embellished the cathedral, adding the now-iconic spire. Hugo's influence extended beyond the written word; his vivid descriptions and compelling themes have inspired countless adaptations in other media, from stage productions to films, ensuring that both his story and the cathedral remain ingrained in popular culture.

Notre-Dame's presence in art is equally profound. The cathedral has been a subject of fascination for painters, engravers, and illustrators since the Middle Ages. Its distinctive silhouette, with its twin towers and delicate tracery, has been immortalized in works by artists such as Camille Corot, whose paintings captured the cathedral's majesty against the backdrop of the Seine. In the Impressionist era, Claude Monet's *Notre-Dame de Paris* series depicted the cathedral bathed in shifting light, emphasizing its ethereal beauty and its connection to the natural world.

Artists have also explored the cathedral's interior, finding inspiration in its play of light and shadow, its soaring arches, and its intricate details. Henri Matisse and Marc Chagall, for example, drew upon the visual language of stained glass—a hallmark of Notre-Dame—in their own explorations of light and color. For these artists, the cathedral was not just a building but a source of creative energy, a space where art and spirituality converged.

The allure of Notre-Dame extends to modern art as well. Contemporary artists have engaged with the cathedral in ways that challenge traditional notions of representation, using it as a symbol of resilience, transformation, and collective memory. After the 2019 fire, artists around the world responded with works that paid homage to Notre-Dame, capturing its beauty and tragedy while imagining its future. These pieces, ranging from sculptures to digital renderings, demonstrate the enduring power of the cathedral to inspire creativity and provoke reflection.

Notre-Dame's influence on music and performance is another dimension of its artistic legacy. The cathedral has been a venue for sacred music for centuries, its acoustics lending themselves to the soaring harmonies of Gregorian chant and choral compositions. Composers such as Camille Saint-Saëns and Olivier Messiaen have drawn inspiration from the spiritual atmosphere of Notre-Dame, creating works that echo its grandeur and mystery. The sound of the cathedral's bells, particularly the great Emmanuel bell, has also become iconic, symbolizing the passage of time and the heartbeat of Paris.

Theatrical adaptations of *The Hunchback of Notre-Dame* have further cemented the cathedral's place in the performing arts. From the dramatic retellings of Hugo's novel to Disney's animated interpretation, Notre-Dame serves as both a literal and symbolic stage, its arches and towers framing tales of love, loss, and redemption. These performances bring new audiences to Notre-Dame's story, ensuring that its legacy endures across generations and cultures.

The cathedral's literary and artistic influence also extends to the realm of poetry. Poets from Charles Baudelaire to T.S. Eliot have invoked Notre-Dame in their works, using it as a symbol of faith, decay, and transcendence. In Eliot's *The Waste Land*, for example, the cathedral serves as a counterpoint to the fragmentation and despair of modern life, offering a vision of continuity and renewal. These poetic reflections capture the paradoxes of Notre-Dame: it is both eternal and fleeting, a structure that endures yet evolves, a monument to both human achievement and divine grace.

In the 21st century, Notre-Dame continues to inspire. The 2019 fire, devastating as it was, has only deepened its significance in art and literature. Writers, artists, and musicians have responded to the tragedy with works that explore themes of loss and resilience, capturing the emotional impact of the fire while celebrating the cathedral's enduring presence. These creations reflect the evolving relationship between Notre-Dame and the world, showing how its legacy adapts to contemporary concerns while remaining rooted in its historical and cultural context.

Notre-Dame's role in art and literature is a testament to its universal appeal. It transcends boundaries of time, place, and medium, offering inspiration to creators from all walks of life. Whether depicted in the words of Victor Hugo, the brushstrokes of Claude Monet, or the melodies of Olivier Messiaen, Notre-Dame remains a source of wonder and meaning, a reminder of the power of human creativity and the enduring connection between art, architecture, and the human spirit.

As the restoration of Notre-Dame progresses, its legacy in art and literature continues to grow. The cathedral's story is far from over; it is a living narrative, one that evolves with each new generation of creators. In this way, Notre-Dame is not just a monument to the past but a beacon for the future, a symbol of resilience and renewal that continues to inspire and transform.

4.Looking Forward: What Notre-Dame Means Today

Notre-Dame de Paris is more than just a building; it is a living symbol of faith, culture, and resilience that has evolved over centuries. The fire of 2019, while devastating, reminded the world of the cathedral's significance and sparked a renewed conversation about its role in the modern age. As Notre-Dame undergoes restoration, the question arises: what does this iconic structure mean to us today, in a world vastly different from the one in which it was conceived?

At its core, Notre-Dame remains a place of spiritual reflection. Built to glorify God and inspire devotion, the cathedral continues to host masses and religious ceremonies, offering a space for prayer and contemplation. For Catholics, it represents a tangible connection to their faith, a sacred site that has stood steadfast through wars, revolutions, and societal change. Even as global trends point to increasing secularism, Notre-Dame retains its spiritual gravitas, drawing visitors who seek solace, inspiration, or simply a moment of quiet in a chaotic world.

But Notre-Dame's meaning extends far beyond its religious roots. It is also a symbol of cultural heritage, a testament to human creativity and ingenuity. Its intricate Gothic architecture, adorned with soaring spires and carved gargoyles, speaks to the skill and vision of the medieval craftsmen who built it. Every stone, every stained-glass window tells a story—not just of a building, but of the people and the era that shaped it. In this sense, Notre-Dame serves as a bridge between past and present, reminding us of the continuity of human experience and the importance of preserving our shared history.

The cathedral's significance as a cultural landmark is perhaps best illustrated by the global response to the 2019 fire. The images of Notre-Dame in flames elicited an outpouring of grief and solidarity from people around the world, many of whom had never set foot inside its walls. This reaction underscored the idea that Notre-Dame belongs not just to Paris or France, but to humanity as a whole. It is a shared treasure, a universal symbol of resilience and beauty that transcends national and cultural boundaries.

In the wake of the fire, Notre-Dame has also come to embody the concept of renewal. The restoration effort, ambitious in scope and meticulous in execution, reflects humanity's determination to rebuild and preserve what is most precious. It is a reminder that even in the face of destruction, there is an opportunity for growth and transformation. This narrative of resilience resonates deeply in a world grappling with its own challenges, from climate change to social inequality. Notre-Dame's restoration is not just about bricks and mortar; it is about hope, unity, and the enduring power of the human spirit.

Notre-Dame's role as an educational and cultural resource has also expanded in recent years. The restoration process has provided new opportunities to explore the cathedral's history, architecture, and artistry. Advanced technologies such as 3D scanning and digital modeling have revealed previously hidden details about its construction, offering fresh insights into the techniques of its medieval builders. These discoveries are being shared with the public through exhibitions, documentaries, and virtual tours, ensuring that Notre-Dame's story reaches a global audience.

The cathedral has also become a focal point for discussions about sustainability and the preservation of cultural heritage in the face of modern challenges. The fire highlighted the vulnerability of historic landmarks, prompting renewed efforts to protect them from environmental and human-made threats. Notre-Dame's restoration incorporates sustainable practices and materials, setting an example for similar projects around the world. This emphasis on sustainability reflects a broader understanding of what it means to preserve heritage—not just for its own sake, but as part of a commitment to future generations.

As Notre-Dame looks to the future, it is also embracing its role as a space for dialogue and connection. The cathedral has always been a gathering place, whether for worshippers, tourists, or locals seeking a quiet moment by the Seine. In the modern era, it continues to serve as a venue for cultural and community events, bringing people together to celebrate art, music, and shared traditions. This inclusivity is essential for ensuring that Notre-Dame remains relevant in a diverse and rapidly changing world.

For many, Notre-Dame is a symbol of Paris itself, embodying the city's history, elegance, and resilience. Its silhouette, reflected in the waters of the Seine, has inspired countless artists, writers, and dreamers. Yet, its meaning is not confined to its physical presence. Notre-Dame represents the ideals of beauty, creativity, and endurance that have defined Paris as a cultural capital for centuries. It is a beacon of inspiration, reminding us of the importance of striving for excellence and preserving what matters most.

Looking forward, Notre-Dame's restoration is an opportunity to reaffirm its significance in a contemporary context. The rebuilt cathedral will not only honor its past but also reflect the values and aspirations of the present. It will continue to be a place of worship, a cultural treasure, and a symbol of resilience, but it will also take on new roles—as a hub for education, a model of sustainability, and a source of inspiration for the next generation.

Notre-Dame's meaning today is multifaceted, shaped by its history and its ongoing restoration. It is a reminder of the power of human creativity, the importance of preserving our shared heritage, and the potential for renewal in the face of adversity. As the cathedral rises from the ashes, it carries with it the hopes and dreams of people around the world, standing as a testament to what we can achieve when we come together to protect and celebrate what we hold dear.

In many ways, Notre-Dame is more than a cathedral; it is a living story, one that continues to unfold with each passing year. Its restoration is not the end of its journey, but the beginning of a new chapter—one that reaffirms its place in the hearts and minds of people everywhere. As we look to the future, Notre-Dame reminds us of the enduring power of beauty, faith, and resilience, offering a vision of hope and renewal that will resonate for generations to come.

Additional Sections

1.Timeline of Notre-Dame's History

The history of Notre-Dame de Paris spans more than 850 years, a timeline rich with milestones that reflect not only the evolution of the cathedral but also the unfolding story of Paris and France itself. From its humble beginnings as a medieval construction site to its status as a global cultural icon, Notre-Dame has been a witness to the triumphs, tragedies, and transformations of the world around it.

1163: The Foundations Are Laid

The story of Notre-Dame begins in 1163, when construction was initiated under the reign of King Louis VII. Maurice de Sully, the Bishop of Paris, envisioned a grand cathedral dedicated to the Virgin Mary, one that would embody the glory of God and reflect the growing power of the Catholic Church. The Île de la Cité, a small island in the Seine River, was chosen as the site, replacing an earlier church that had stood there for centuries. Legend holds that Pope Alexander III laid the cornerstone, though records are unclear. What is certain is that the construction of Notre-Dame marked the beginning of one of the most ambitious architectural projects of the Middle Ages.

13th Century: Completion of the Cathedral

Construction of Notre-Dame took nearly two centuries to complete, a testament to the challenges of medieval building techniques and the grandeur of the vision. By 1250, the primary structure, including the nave, choir, and two towers, was largely finished. The famous flying buttresses, a hallmark of Gothic architecture, were added in the late 13th century to support the cathedral's massive stone walls. These innovative structures allowed the builders to create the soaring ceilings and expansive stained-glass windows that define Notre-Dame's interior. The cathedral's west facade, with its iconic rose window and intricately carved portals, was completed during this period, becoming a symbol of Parisian artistry.

14th–16th Centuries: A Center of Religious and Cultural Life

As one of the largest and most magnificent cathedrals in Europe, Notre-Dame became a focal point of religious and civic life in medieval Paris. It hosted coronations, royal weddings, and other significant events, including the crowning of Henry VI of England as King of France in 1431 during the Hundred Years' War. The cathedral's grandeur and central location made it a natural gathering place for the people of Paris, solidifying its role as the spiritual heart of the city.

1789–1799: The French Revolution

The French Revolution brought dramatic changes to Notre-Dame. Seen as a symbol of the monarchy and the Church's power, the cathedral was desecrated and repurposed as the Temple of Reason. Many of its treasures, including religious relics and statues, were destroyed or looted. The famous statues of the biblical kings on the facade were mistaken for French monarchs and beheaded by revolutionaries. The Great Emmanuel Bell, however, was spared, and the building itself narrowly avoided demolition. By the end of the revolution, Notre-Dame was in a state of disrepair, a shadow of its former glory.

1804: Napoleon Bonaparte's Coronation

Notre-Dame's fortunes changed with the rise of Napoleon Bonaparte. In 1804, he chose the cathedral as the site of his coronation as Emperor of the French, an event that signaled the return of grandeur to the neglected structure. Napoleon's decision underscored Notre-Dame's symbolic importance as a national monument, linking it to the heritage of France's monarchy and its new empire. This event marked the beginning of a renewed appreciation for the cathedral, setting the stage for its restoration.

1844–1864: Restoration by Viollet-le-Duc

Victor Hugo's *The Hunchback of Notre-Dame*, published in 1831, played a pivotal role in rekindling public interest in the cathedral. The novel's vivid descriptions of Notre-Dame, combined with its critique of neglect, inspired a movement to restore the aging structure. In 1844, the architect Eugène Viollet-le-Duc was commissioned to lead the restoration. Over two decades, Viollet-le-Duc and his team painstakingly repaired and enhanced Notre-Dame, adding the now-iconic spire and restoring many of its sculptures and stained glass. While some criticized his approach as overly imaginative, his work ensured the cathedral's survival and revitalized its status as a masterpiece of Gothic architecture.

20th Century: Wars and Resilience

During World War I and World War II, Notre-Dame endured the tumult of conflict but emerged largely unscathed. The cathedral's bells rang out to celebrate the liberation of Paris in 1944, a moment that underscored its role as a symbol of French identity and resilience. In the decades that followed, Notre-Dame became an increasingly popular tourist destination, attracting millions of visitors each year.

April 15, 2019: The Devastating Fire

One of the darkest days in Notre-Dame's history came on April 15, 2019, when a fire broke out beneath the roof during restoration work. The blaze quickly engulfed the wooden framework, known as "the forest," and caused the collapse of the spire. For hours, firefighters battled the flames, saving the twin towers and much of the cathedral's interior, including its precious relics and stained glass. The fire was a tragedy that shocked the world, but it also galvanized a global effort to restore Notre-Dame, with donations pouring in from every corner of the globe.

2020–Present: Restoration and Renewal

The restoration of Notre-Dame began almost immediately after the fire, with a focus on stabilizing the structure and preserving what remained. Modern technology, including 3D scanning and advanced materials, has played a crucial role in the reconstruction process. The decision to rebuild the spire as a replica of Viollet-le-Duc's design reflects a commitment to historical accuracy, while the integration of sustainable practices ensures that the cathedral is prepared for future challenges. The project has become a symbol of resilience and renewal, demonstrating humanity's ability to overcome adversity and protect its cultural treasures.

True to French President Emmanuel Macron's ambitious declaration, the major restoration work is set to be completed within five years. Notre-Dame is scheduled to reopen on **December 8, 2024**, a moment eagerly anticipated by people around the globe. On that day, public access to the cathedral will resume, and the grand reopening will be marked by a live broadcast streamed worldwide. This event will not only celebrate the completion of a monumental restoration effort but also reaffirm Notre-Dame's role as a global symbol of faith, culture, and unity.

Looking Forward: A Living Legacy

As Notre-Dame nears its reopening, its timeline continues to grow. The cathedral's history is not just a record of its past; it is a testament to its enduring significance. Each era has left its mark on Notre-Dame, shaping it into a living monument that reflects the values, challenges, and aspirations of humanity. Its survival through fire and revolution, its restoration through art and innovation, and its ability to inspire people across the globe make Notre-Dame a symbol of what we hold most dear.

2.Architectural Glossary of Gothic Terms

Understanding the architectural marvel of Notre-Dame de Paris requires familiarity with the vocabulary of Gothic architecture—a style that emerged in 12th-century France and revolutionized building techniques and design. Below is a detailed glossary of key Gothic architectural terms, with explanations that highlight their significance and application in Notre-Dame.

Ribbed Vault

A ribbed vault is a structural framework of intersecting arched ribs that support a vaulted ceiling. In Gothic architecture, ribbed vaults allowed builders to construct taller and more expansive interiors. At Notre-Dame, the ribbed vaults are integral to the cathedral's soaring nave and aisles, distributing the weight of the stone ceiling while creating a visually striking pattern of lines that draw the eye upward, emphasizing the verticality that characterizes Gothic design.

Flying Buttress

The flying buttress is one of the most iconic innovations of Gothic architecture. These external supports transfer the weight of the roof and upper walls away from the building, channeling it to ground-level piers. At Notre-Dame, the flying buttresses are particularly notable on the eastern end, where their elegant arcs not only provide essential structural support but also add a sense of grace and complexity to the exterior design.

Pointed Arch

The pointed arch is a defining feature of Gothic architecture, replacing the rounded arches of Romanesque buildings. Its shape allows for greater height and flexibility in design, distributing weight more efficiently. Pointed arches are used extensively in Notre-Dame, from the grand portals of the facade to the interior arcades, enhancing the cathedral's sense of height and grandeur.

Rose Window

A rose window is a large, circular stained-glass window, often featuring intricate radial patterns and vibrant colors. Notre-Dame's rose windows, particularly the north and south transept windows, are masterpieces of medieval craftsmanship. These windows not only illuminate the interior with colorful light but also depict biblical stories and saints, serving as visual sermons for the faithful.

Tracery

Tracery refers to the stone framework that supports and divides the glass in a Gothic window. At Notre-Dame, the delicate tracery of the rose windows creates intricate patterns that resemble lace. This feature exemplifies the Gothic emphasis on lightness and ornamentation, transforming functional elements into works of art.

Clerestory

The clerestory is the uppermost section of the nave walls, featuring a row of windows that bring natural light into the interior. At Notre-Dame, the clerestory windows are part of the tripartite elevation, which also includes the arcade and triforium. These windows flood the interior with light, creating a sense of ethereal beauty and connecting the worshipper to the divine.

Triforium

The triforium is a shallow, decorative gallery located between the arcade and the clerestory in a Gothic cathedral. At Notre-Dame, the triforium runs along the length of the nave and choir, providing visual balance and adding depth to the interior design. Though not functional as a walkway, it serves as an architectural element that enhances the cathedral's layered aesthetic.

Spire

A spire is a tall, pointed structure that rises above the roofline, often serving as a focal point in Gothic architecture. Notre-Dame's original spire, designed by Eugène Viollet-le-Duc in the 19th century, was a modern addition that complemented the medieval design. Tragically lost in the 2019 fire, it is being rebuilt as part of the current restoration effort, reaffirming its role as a symbol of the cathedral's resilience and aspiration.

Gargoyle

Gargoyles are carved stone figures that serve both decorative and functional purposes, acting as water spouts to direct rain away from the building. The gargoyles of Notre-Dame are particularly famous, their grotesque and fantastical forms capturing the imagination of visitors and adding a sense of mystery to the cathedral. While their primary role was practical, their exaggerated expressions and animalistic features are an example of the medieval fascination with the grotesque.

Grotesque

Distinct from gargoyles, grotesques are ornamental sculptures that do not serve as water spouts. Found throughout Notre-Dame, these carved figures often depict mythical creatures, demons, and strange hybrid forms. Their purpose is both decorative and symbolic, serving as reminders of the spiritual battle between good and evil and reflecting the medieval worldview.

Finial

A finial is a decorative, often pointed, ornament that tops spires, pinnacles, or gables. At Notre-Dame, finials are found crowning the flying buttresses and other architectural elements, contributing to the cathedral's intricate silhouette and adding an additional layer of detail to its design.

Portal

A portal is a grand entrance, often framed by ornate carvings and sculptures. The western facade of Notre-Dame features three magnificent portals: the Portal of the Virgin, the Portal of the Last Judgment, and the Portal of Saint Anne. Each portal is adorned with detailed sculptures depicting biblical scenes and figures, offering a visual narrative to those entering the cathedral.

Nave

The nave is the central, longitudinal space of the cathedral, where worshippers gather. At Notre-Dame, the nave is a breathtaking space defined by its ribbed vaults, towering columns, and clerestory windows. Its sheer size and height evoke a sense of the divine, drawing visitors into a sacred realm.

Choir

The choir is the area of the cathedral where the clergy conduct religious services. Located beyond the nave and near the altar, the choir at Notre-Dame is richly adorned with sculptures, carved stalls, and an ornate screen. It serves as the spiritual heart of the cathedral, emphasizing its primary function as a house of worship.

Apse

The apse is the semicircular or polygonal termination of the choir, often featuring chapels and large windows. At Notre-Dame, the apse is a masterpiece of design, with radiating chapels and a series of flying buttresses that provide both support and visual drama. The apse's layout exemplifies the Gothic focus on creating harmonious and inspiring spaces.

Pinnacle

A pinnacle is a pointed ornament atop buttresses or other vertical elements, often weighted to add stability to the structure. The pinnacles of Notre-Dame are not only functional but also decorative, contributing to the cathedral's vertical emphasis and ornate aesthetic.

3.Bibliography and Recommended Resources

Notre-Dame de Paris has been the subject of extensive study, inspiring countless books, articles, and multimedia resources. For readers who wish to delve deeper into the history, architecture, and cultural significance of this iconic cathedral, the following bibliography and recommended resources provide a curated selection of authoritative works and engaging materials. These resources span historical analyses, architectural studies, artistic explorations, and literary masterpieces, offering a comprehensive understanding of Notre-Dame's enduring legacy.

Books on Notre-Dame's History and Architecture

1. **Victor Hugo, *The Hunchback of Notre-Dame (Notre-Dame de Paris)***

First published in 1831, Victor Hugo's novel is a seminal work that brought international attention to Gothic architecture and played a crucial role in the preservation of Notre-Dame. While fictional, the novel's vivid descriptions of the cathedral and its historical context offer invaluable insights into its significance during the 19th century.

2. **Andrew Tallon, *Notre-Dame de Paris: Architecture and the Spirit of the Gothic***

Tallon's pioneering work combines historical research with cutting-edge laser scanning technology to explore Notre-Dame's construction and design. His detailed analysis reveals the ingenuity of medieval builders and the cathedral's architectural evolution.

3. **Alain Erlande-Brandenburg, *Notre-Dame de Paris***

Written by a renowned French historian, this book provides a concise yet thorough history of Notre-Dame, from its construction to its role in French cultural identity. The book includes beautiful illustrations and photographs, making it an accessible introduction for general readers.

4. **Eugène Viollet-le-Duc, *Dictionnaire raisonné de l'architecture française du XIe au XVIe siècle***

Viollet-le-Duc's monumental work remains a cornerstone of Gothic architectural scholarship. His insights into the restoration of Notre-Dame, including the addition of the iconic spire, provide essential historical context for understanding the cathedral's design.

Artistic and Cultural Perspectives

1. **Camille Corot and Claude Monet: Art Inspired by Notre-Dame**

For art enthusiasts, collections featuring works by Corot, Monet, and other artists who painted Notre-Dame offer a visual exploration of its aesthetic impact. The interplay of light and shadow captured in their works highlights the cathedral's timeless beauty.

2. **Jean Gimpel, *The Cathedral Builders***

This book examines the lives of the medieval craftsmen who constructed Europe's great cathedrals, including Notre-Dame.

Gimpel's work offers a human perspective on the labor and artistry behind these monumental structures.

3. T.S. Eliot, *The Waste Land*

Although not exclusively about Notre-Dame, Eliot's poem references the cathedral and its cultural symbolism, using it as a metaphor for continuity amidst modern chaos. It provides a literary lens through which to appreciate Notre-Dame's broader impact.

Historical and Restoration Focus

1. Elizabeth Boyle, *Saving Notre-Dame: The Effort to Rebuild a French Icon*

Published in the aftermath of the 2019 fire, this book documents the global response to the tragedy and the ongoing restoration efforts. Boyle interviews key figures involved in the project, offering a behind-the-scenes look at the challenges and triumphs of rebuilding.

2. Colin Cunningham, *Gothic Design and the Medieval Spirit*

This book explores the principles of Gothic design, with specific case studies on Notre-Dame and other cathedrals. Cunningham provides context for understanding the architectural innovations that made Notre-Dame a masterpiece of its era.

3. Ministère de la Culture, *Notre-Dame de Paris: La Restauration d'un Monument Vivant*

This official publication from the French Ministry of Culture offers detailed reports and photographs from the ongoing restoration project, providing a firsthand account of the work being done to preserve the cathedral.

Multimedia and Online Resources

1. The Virtual Notre-Dame Project

Created by a team of researchers and technologists, this digital reconstruction of Notre-Dame allows users to explore the cathedral in its pre-fire state. This immersive experience is particularly valuable for understanding the spatial and aesthetic qualities of Gothic architecture.

2. National Geographic Documentaries

National Geographic's coverage of the 2019 fire and subsequent restoration includes documentaries and articles that provide expert commentary and stunning visuals, making it an accessible resource for general audiences.

3. The Notre-Dame Official Website

The cathedral's official website offers updates on restoration progress, historical timelines, and information on visiting Notre-Dame once it reopens. It is a reliable source for current developments and public engagement.

4. Google Arts & Culture: Notre-Dame de Paris

This online platform offers a virtual tour of the cathedral and curated exhibits about its history, art, and restoration. It is an excellent resource for remote exploration and education.

Recommended Academic Journals and Articles

1. The Journal of Gothic Studies

This peer-reviewed journal includes scholarly articles on Gothic architecture, with several issues dedicated to Notre-Dame. Topics range from its medieval construction to its influence on later architectural movements.

2. "Notre-Dame de Paris: Engineering a Gothic Icon" (Journal of Architectural History)

This article delves into the structural innovations that defined Notre-Dame, highlighting the engineering achievements that made its construction possible.

3. "The 2019 Notre-Dame Fire: Lessons in Preservation" (Heritage Science)

Focused on the aftermath of the fire, this article examines the challenges of restoring historic landmarks in the modern era, using Notre-Dame as a case study.

Conclusion

This bibliography and list of recommended resources provide a wealth of material for those who wish to explore Notre-Dame from every angle. Whether your interest lies in its history, architecture, art, or restoration, these works offer deep insights and rich perspectives, ensuring a deeper appreciation of this iconic cathedral and its enduring legacy.

Afterword

Notre-Dame de Paris stands as a testament to the resilience of human creativity, faith, and determination. From its first stone laid in the 12th century to its near-destruction and subsequent restoration in the 21st, this iconic cathedral has captured the hearts and imaginations of people across the globe. It has weathered revolutions, wars, and natural disasters, each event adding new layers to its rich and complex story.

Writing this book has been an incredible journey—a way to reflect on the enduring legacy of Notre-Dame and what it represents in our rapidly changing world. It is more than an architectural marvel; it is a living symbol of hope, unity, and renewal. The 2019 fire was a tragic reminder of the fragility of our cultural heritage, but it was also a catalyst for global solidarity, inspiring millions to contribute to its restoration.

This book is not just about Notre-Dame's history, architecture, and influence—it is about how it continues to inspire us to protect, preserve, and reimagine what we hold dear. Whether you are drawn to its intricate Gothic design, its role in literature and art, or its spiritual significance, I hope this book has deepened your appreciation for Notre-Dame and the lessons it offers us.

As the cathedral prepares to reopen, I am reminded of its timeless message: that even in the face of destruction, renewal is possible. Notre-Dame's story is far from over, and I am grateful to have shared a small part of it with you.

Thank you for joining me on this journey. I invite you to reflect on what Notre-Dame means to you and to carry its lessons of resilience and beauty into your own life.

Acknowledgments

This book would not have been possible without the support and inspiration of countless individuals. I would like to express my deepest gratitude to the researchers, historians, architects, and artisans whose work has illuminated the history and restoration of Notre-Dame. Their dedication and expertise have been invaluable in shaping this narrative.

To my family and friends, thank you for your encouragement and patience throughout this project. Your belief in my vision kept me motivated and focused.

Lastly, to the readers—your curiosity and passion for learning about Notre-

Dame inspire me to continue exploring and sharing stories of our shared heritage. Thank you for allowing me to be part of your journey.

About the Author

I am an author and historian with a deep passion for exploring the intersections of art, architecture, and culture. My goal is to bring history to life for modern readers by delving into the stories behind iconic landmarks and the people who shaped them. Through my work, I hope to foster a greater appreciation for our shared cultural heritage and its continued relevance in today's world.

Invitation for Feedback

Your thoughts and insights are incredibly valuable to me. If this book has inspired you, taught you something new, or sparked questions, I would love to hear from you. Feedback not only helps me grow as a writer but also strengthens the connection between author and reader.

You can reach me at [Your Email Address] or through [Your Social Media Handles]. Reviews and comments on platforms like [Amazon, Goodreads, etc.] are also deeply appreciated—they help others discover this book and join the conversation.

Thank you for taking the time to read this work. Your engagement and support mean the world to me. Let's keep the dialogue about Notre-Dame and its enduring legacy alive.

Date of Completion
November 2024
Author
Louis Martin